THIS *Charge* THIS GENERATION

COULD THIS BE THE *Generation* THAT BRINGS ABOUT *Change* IN THE EARTH?

1 Timothy 1:18 and 2:1-4

JOEL LANDIS

Unless otherwise indicated, all Scripture quotations are from the *New King James Version*®, © 1982 by Thomas Nelson, Inc. Used by permission. All rights reserved.

Scripture quotations marked (KJV) are from the authorized King James Version.

Scripture quotations marked (NAS) are from the NEW AMERICAN STANDARD BIBLE Copyright © 1960, 1962, 1963, 1968, 1971, 1973, 1975, 1977, 1995 by The Lockman Foundation. Used by permission.

Scripture quotations marked (NCV) are from the New Century Version © 1987, 1988, 1991 by Word Publishing, a division of Thomas Nelson, Inc. All rights reserved.

Scripture quotations marked (Interlinear) are from the Interlinear Greek-English New Testament, Literal English Translation © 1958 by Samuel Bagster and Sons LTD

Scripture quotations marked (NLT) are from the *Holy Bible,* New Living Translation, copyright © 1996. Used by permission of Tyndale House Publishers, Inc., Wheaton, Illinois 60189. All rights reserved.

Scripture quotations marked (Message) are from *The Message* by Eugene H. Peterson, copyright © 1993, 1994, 1995, 1996, 2000, 2001, 2002. Used by permission of NavPress Publishing Group. All rights reserved.

Emphasis added to Scriptural references is the author's own.

THIS CHARGE...THIS GENERATION:
Could This Be the Generation That Brings About Change in the Earth?

ISBN **0-9763800-0-5**

Printed in the United States of America

Orison Publishing
PO Box 188
Grantham, PA 17027
Ph: 717-433-7985 Fax: 717-427-1525

Visit www.Amazon.com to order additional copies of this book.

Dedication

To my three beautiful girls: my wife Chris and my two daughters Laura and Caroline.

God's dreams do come true!

This charge I commit to you, son Timothy, according to the prophecies previously made concerning you, that by them you may wage the good warfare...

Therefore I exhort first of all that supplications, prayers, intercessions, and giving of thanks be made for all men, for kings and all who are in authority, that we may lead a quiet and peaceable life in all godliness and reverence. For this is good and acceptable in the sight of God our Savior, who desires all men to be saved and to come to the knowledge of the truth.

1 Timothy 1:18, and 2:1-4

Acknowledgments

Special thanks go to:

My wife Chris, for all the hours she gave to this adventure, putting my handwritten words over into the computer and in that same process making it all make sense.

Gene Hollick, for being a good "father" in the faith and sharing with me about our Christian heritage in America.

My in-laws Bob and Junie Bartmess and my brother Dave Landis, for your assistance in checking out this material.

Those who read the manuscript and gave their endorsements. I am so honored.

R.W. Schambach, a lifelong friend of my earthly father, John Landis. Thank you so much for the kind words.

Mel Gibson, for *The Passion*. I do not believe in coincidences; God is going after this generation.

Orison Publishers and Marsha Blessing, for doing such a great job helping us with this book.

Jeanette Sprecher, for great editing work.

My youngest daughter Caroline, for helping me name this book *This Charge...This Generation.*

The Lord Jesus, for giving me this dream and bringing it to pass. Thank You for all the wonderful people You provided to bring this all together in Your time and plan. This all belongs to You; this is Your charge, this is Your generation.

Endorsements

"Joel gave me the manuscript of his latest book and now I am delighted to give him my wholehearted endorsement for a job well done. This book is both a biblical and a practical handbook for Christians everywhere to partner with God to see His kingdom come—in our lives, our churches, and our cities. A real faith-building tool for fruit-bearing Christians."

–Larry Tomczak
Christian leader and author
Christ The King Church of Greater Atlanta

"Joel's book is a timely challenge to this generation of believers. With the increasing intensity of spiritual warfare, he offers balanced, biblical battle plans. A seasoned warrior himself, Joel writes with deep convictions and practical wisdom.

"Those desiring to make the most of every opportunity will greatly appreciate these powerful pages of encouragement. Like the sons of Issachar, we need to be a generation of those who understand the times and know what we have been called to do. This book will help in that process."

–Dave Hess
Pastor, Christ Community Church, Camp Hill, PA

"I believe that anyone who reads *This Charge...This Generation* will be inspired to put more effort and time into his or her prayer life. This book reveals to us not only how to pray for our nation and its leadership, but also why we are to pray for those who are in authority. Joel takes the Scriptures and ties the relationship of the spiritual realm to the natural realm in a very organized and complete fashion. Each chapter of the book develops God's will in the area of prayer through line upon line expounding of Scripture.

"This book would be especially beneficial to those who are sensitive to God's heart in the realm of intercession. In every generation, God has called people to 'know the times and the seasons' of their day. After reading this book, you will be challenged to not just give in to the pressures of the age, but to declare God's will to be done in the earth as it is done in heaven. *This Charge...This Generation*, should be required reading for every saint of God, but especially for those who share in the leadership of the church of the Lord Jesus Christ."

–David R. Landis, D.Min.
Word of Grace Ministries, Harrisburg, PA

"Joel Landis is an incredible student of the Word of God. His wisdom and insight in *This Charge...This Generation* will enhance and encourage any believer's life."

–Pastor Jacob Aranza
Our Savior's Church, Lafayette, LA
Author, communicator,
and Editorial Advisory Board member of *New Man* Magazine

Table of Contents

Foreword

I have been a part of many generations in the past and seen the power of God demonstrated down through the years. Signs and wonders and miracles have taken place because believers went forth and were obedient to the command of Christ. I have seen change come, not only in the world, but also in the church of Jesus Christ.

The Lord has kept me alive all these years to now, which I believe is the time of the final generation—the generation that will see the greatest change in the world, in the church and in the believer who will do what God has commanded them to do. This book by Joel Landis, *This Charge... This Generation*, will help equip the believer to finish the work that Christ commanded us to do. I recommend that every believer get hold of this book and read it until it gets into your spirit so that you can be a part of the final change before the coming of our Lord and Savior Jesus Christ.

When the church was born 2,000 years ago, 120 believers obeyed the command of Christ and planted this Gospel in every part of the then-known world. Since then the church has been a failure at times. But I personally believe that the generation we see today is going to come alive and finish the work that Jesus commanded us to do—and *YOU* can be a part of this change that's coming in the body of Christ today.

So accept the charge and be a part of this generation that will bring back Jesus.

R.W. Schambach

Evangelist

Introduction: This Generation

One generation passes away, and another generation comes; but the earth abides forever. Ecclesiastes 1:4

Therefore it is also contained in the Scripture, "Behold, I lay in Zion a chief cornerstone, elect, precious, and he who believes on Him will by no means be put to shame." Therefore, to you who believe, He is precious; but to those who are disobedient, "The stone which the builders rejected has become the chief cornerstone," and "A stone of stumbling and a rock of offense." They stumble, being disobedient to the word, to which they also were appointed. But you are a chosen generation, a royal priesthood, a holy nation, His own special people, that you may proclaim the praises of Him who called you out of darkness into His marvelous light; who once were not a people but are now the people of God, who had not obtained mercy but now have obtained mercy. 1 Peter 2:6-10

A millennium has come to an end and a new one begun. Everyone expected something "big" to happen on January 1, 2000. However, the "millennium bug" was not all that it was feared to be; it turned out to be only a "stink bug." Y2K came and went without the world coming to an end. Something's wrong here, many thought. Maybe the millennium really doesn't end until December 31, 2000? Maybe January 1, 2001, is the real time for the world as we know it to end?

Again the predictors of doom and gloom struck out. The new year came in and the old one went out rather peacefully despite all the false prophets and their fear-filled words that caused many to make decisions based on the word of men rather than the Word of God.

It seems that many people have forgotten the importance of hearing the Word of God and instead follow the word of man as the hope of their salvation in the sweet here and now. The words of Jesus, *"When the Son of Man comes, will He really find faith on the earth?"* (Luke 18:8) have been put to the test. I believe our faith has been challenged. My faith was and is still being challenged by this question, and I have decided that no matter what, when Jesus comes He *will* find faith on the earth—in me.

Have you ever had an "illumination"? Something you saw or heard on the outside suddenly exploded on the inside, in your heart or in your mind, or both? Did you ever get a "revelation" of something like the disciple Simon did the day that Father God revealed to him in his heart (spirit) that Jesus is the Christ? I experienced such a moment during the summer of 2001. One of the lay ministers in our home church was doing a study on our "Christian heritage." It was very informative and well-documented; the research was extensive; and best of all the speaker was sharing the facts not just from a bunch of books but from his heart. He, being a godly man and a patriot, challenged us not only to be informed and aware of what is going on in this great land, but also to do our part as Christians in voicing our concerns by writing letters to our congressmen, senators and the President himself. He urged us to vote and elect Christian leaders; to support Christian coalition-type of groups; and to pray for our leaders every day.

In his presentation he talked about how in June of 1962 with the *Engel v. Vitale* case, the Supreme Court of the United States of America forbade the inclusion of prayer and Bible recitations in daily student life by striking down *non-compulsory* school prayer and Bible reading from the public schools in New York. Then within a year, by June.17, 1963, the Supreme Court removed *non-compulsory* prayer with its decision in two cases, the *Abington v. Sthhempp* case and *Murray v. Curlett* case. These decisions have since come to be interpreted as forbidding the inclusion of Christian religion in major activities of daily student life. Never before in the history of our nation had any branch of our government taken such a stand, "preferring those who believe in no religion over those who do believe."[1]

Through those decisions, 30 million students and more than 2 million teachers were barred from participating in what previously had been available to students all across our nation.[2]

Before these decisions were made, school students in various states across our country had been participating in opening exercises that included Bible reading and recitation of the Lord's prayer or other prayers, such as the following one composed by the state board of regents in New York:

> "Almighty God, we acknowledge our dependance upon thee, and we beg thy blessings upon us, our parents, our teachers, and our country."

Since 1962— when Bible reading and prayer were removed from our schools—it seems that the morals and standards of our nation have gone on a downward spiral. That year brought in a no-holds barred effort to remove God Himself from schools and public places. (By the way, no one, including the devil, can remove God.) It was the beginning of a moral decline in this nation that, since its Declaration of Independence, depended upon God as the source of its strength. Even our currency has said "In God We Trust" since 1865.

After hearing about all that had happened through the Supreme Court's rulings in 1962 and 1963, I began to see in my mind's eye what was really going on here. Some things that I had known for years started to click and fall into place concerning the way these events came about over the last four decades. I got an illumination!

I began to think back over the 1980's when my wife and I, with others helping us, traveled around the country giving public presentations or seminars on "Rock and Roll and the Occult." We spoke in churches, coffee houses, schools, colleges, homes, theaters, community parks and even a few prisons, to anyone who would give us their ear. We also did a few radio and television interviews.

In our seminars, one of the first things I always talked about was the "British Invasion" of the early 1960's. That was when the Beatles and the Rolling Stones came to the United States from Great Britain with a new sound and ideology in rock and roll music that revolutionized that generation. At the time I was giving those seminars, I was completely unaware of the Supreme Court's removal of prayer and Bible reading from our schools just prior to this new revolution among the young people of the day.

Looking back now, I can see that Satan was at work using men and women in courtrooms, both plaintiffs and some of the judges themselves, to bring about an attempt to destroy this nation. This was a satanic attack against God and Christianity itself, and the devil waged his war using people. In an interview in 1964, Madelyn Murray was quoted as saying, "I've always believed I could do anything better or faster or both than anyone else. And I've never had any real competition. I wish I did. I'd like to lose in a good, tough fight. I guess fighting God and God's spokesmen is sort of the ultimate, isn't it?"[3]

Within two years of the Supreme Court's decisions to remove prayer and Bible reading from our schools, the Beatles arrived in the United States when they appeared on *The Ed Sullivan Show* in February 1964. That same year the Beatles' press officer Derek Taylor, who was traveling with them, said this about them: "It's incredible, absolutely incredible. Here are these four boys from Liverpool. They're rude, they're profane, they're vulgar, and they've taken over the world. It's as if they'd founded a new religion. They're completely anti-Christ. I mean, I'm anti-Christ as well, but they're so anti-Christ they shock me, which isn't an easy thing."[4]

Just two years later the Beatles' own John Lennon said, "Christianity will go. It will vanish and shrink. I needn't argue about that: I'm right and I will be proved right. We're more popular than Jesus now."[5]

When Satan saw that he had succeeded in removing prayer and the reading of God's Word in our schools, he immediately used the British Invasion to bring into America a revolution of thoughts and ideas that, up until this time, were never dreamed of in this nation.

In 1967 the Beatles came out with their most famous album, called *Sergeant Pepper's Lonely Hearts Club Band.* The album cover included the face of a man named Aleister Crowley, who was a practitioner of magic (or witchcraft) in the twentieth century. Many called him the "wickedest man in the world," and he called himself "666, The Great Beast."[6] Though he died in 1947, his teachings on satanic ideas and theologies continue through his writings and disciples. His motto was pretty much a summation of his teachings: "Do what thou wilt shall be the whole of the law." Among those checking out his teachings were a number of famous rock stars, including members of The Rolling Stones.

Jimmy Page of "Stairway to Heaven" fame bought Crowley's old mansion in Scotland as well as his own occult bookstore, which he dedicated to Aleister Crowley. In the 1970's a lot of youth, including myself, were playing and singing "Stairway to Heaven," even at times in our churches, completely unaware that this song's heaven was not the Christian Heaven.

While Aleister Crowley was still living, he was actually banned from the United States because of his perversion and the satanic theology that he was preaching. However, in 1967 he "came into" the record stores and the homes of America through the Beatles' album. The crowd of faces on that album cover also included Karl Marx and five miscellaneous "gurus" of Eastern religions. At the bottom of the album cover was a doll that had printed on it, "Welcome the Rolling Stones." Ringo Starr said of that album cover, "We just thought we would like to put together a lot of people we like and admire."[6] That same year, the Rolling Stones released their album in America called *Their Satanic Majesty's Request*, and they included pictures of two of the Beatles on the cover. Obviously the Beatles and the Rolling Stones were connecting in some way, and I believe it was because they were rejecting Christianity while still searching for spiritual things. Then they were using their music as a tool to communicate those ideas.

I find it amazing that that album was not banned, but prayer was. The order of those events is significant, I believe. With the removal of prayer and Bible reading from the daily instruction in the lives of children and youth, Satan brought in an onslaught of sexual immorality, drugs and false religion.

He used music to carry a message that would replace truth with a lie, morals with immorality, purity with promiscuity and rebellion against all that previously had been prayed for in our classrooms each and every day.

Jimi Hendrix said this about rock music at the end of the decade of the 1960's: "Atmospheres are going to come through music because music is a spiritual thing of its own...You can hypnotize people...And when you get people at that weakest point you can preach into the subconscious what [you] want to say."[8]

Within ten years of those Supreme Court decisions going into effect, the airwaves of the whole music scene had become a wide-open medium for Satan, whom the Bible calls *"the prince of the power of the air"* (Ephesians 2:2), to put into the minds of people a message that would draw a generation further and further from the truth and standards of God's Word.

John Lennon later released a solo album called *Imagine*. The title song said,

"Imagine there's no heaven
It's easy if you try
No hell below us
Above us only sky
Imagine all the people
Living for today...

...and no religion too...

You may say I'm a dreamer
But I'm not the only one
I hope someday you'll join us
And the world will be as one."[9]

John Lennon's song seems to be an effort to erase God and the truth about Heaven, Hell and accountability to God as our source of life and our standard for decision-making. This song was number one throughout the United States of America and still continues to be played on rock and roll stations and in stores and other public places on a regular basis, even after all these years.

However, God is restoring in the airwaves of America the whole idea of what the song "Imagine" attempted to strip from the souls of a generation. The contemporary Christian music group called MercyMe has released a hit song that is played on Christian radio and, amazingly, on a lot of pop and country music stations. It also has become popular in mainstream music as well. The song is called "I Can Only Imagine," and it encourages us to imagine what Heaven will be like when we find ourselves in the place where we will stand before Almighty God, when this life as we know it comes to an end. I don't believe this is a coincidence. The lyrics say,

I can only imagine
What it will be like
When I walk by Your side
I can only imagine
What my eyes will see
When Your face is before me
I can only imagine.

Surrounded by Your glory, what will my heart feel
Will I dance for You Jesus, or in awe of You be still
Will I stand in Your presence, or to my knees will I fall
Will I sing hallelujah, will I be able to speak at all
I can only imagine.

I can only imagine
When that day comes
And I find myself standing in the Son
I can only imagine
When all I will do
Is forever, forever worship You
I can only imagine.[10]

One thing I have learned over the years is this: Men and women are not our enemies. In the 1960's the Beatles and Madalyn Murray [O'Hare] and others were not our enemies. Our true enemy was behind the scenes manipulating, controlling, influencing and implementing his plans and schemes through the lives of men in this world. Christians, we must come to the realization that we *"do not wrestle against flesh and blood, but against principalities, against powers, against the rulers of the darkness of this age, against spiritual hosts of wickedness"* (Ephesians 6:12). I believe that, as Christians, we must take the Gospel (the Good News) to the people God has placed in our lives. It is our responsibility in this generation to ask God to save the lives of those whom He puts on our hearts, to break the power of Satan and his strongholds over them—whether that stronghold is in their hearts, souls or bodies—and to commit ourselves to pray for them (persevering in it) until change comes in their lives. Even those like John Lennon.

I believe that 1962 was the beginning of a falling away from God in America from the government and leadership on down. In July of 2001 I began to see that because God's principles were removed in America, things seemingly have continued to grow worse. If you add up the years from 1962 to 2002, you will see that we have come to an end of a 40-year time period. Many times throughout the Bible a "generation" is a period of 40 years. So if 1962 was the beginning of a generation going away from God and His standards in America, what will the next generation bring to pass?

I believe that if you remove prayer and Bible reading from your personal life, you, like America, will have your own personal "moral decline." God wants us to bring about change in America. It must begin in our own personal lives and our families and then spread to others. I believe that the power of prayer can change things. It can change people's lives. It can even change Supreme Court decisions. It can change anything if God is involved in it! Jesus Himself said that *"with God all things are possible"* (Mark 10:27).

As this past generation ends, we stand on the threshold of a new generation. Will we be just another generation like the book of Ecclesiastes speaks about (*"one generation passes away, and another generation comes"*), or will we be as the book of 1 Peter says, that generation that believes on Jesus and is not disobedient to the Word? Can the church at this hour be a chosen generation, a royal priesthood, a holy nation? It is time for us to proclaim the praises of Him who called us out of darkness into His marvelous light!

On September 11, 2001, as a generation was coming to a close, a terrible tragedy happened in New York, Pennsylvania and Washington, D.C. I don't need to tell you the story. We all have heard about it and our lives have been and will continue to be changed by the events that happened that day. In one day, prayer was brought back into our schools and other public institutions. In one day, even though tragedy had struck, I believe that this nation once again fell to its knees in a time of need and despair. Do you remember the day? Did you find yourself in a place of prayer? Did you find yourself reading God's Word?

I do not believe God caused all that loss of life, but in the aftermath of those terrorist attacks He called the saints of God to go forth in the power of prayer to see Him bring about change in this world. It seems that we as humans are continually waiting on God, but in actuality He is waiting for us. He wants us to get involved in His plan. He is calling us into the harvest fields. This is a new generation. I believe that this can be a generation like the one spoken of in Psalm 24:6, the one that seeks after God. The year 2003 marked a time of new beginnings. Stop waiting for God. Stop making Him wait on you. Let's get on with the program. Let's be a generation that prays, that brings about change, that recognizes the true enemy and wages a good warfare against him.

We must walk in God's love toward man. As we begin this new generation, what are you going to do?

Endnotes

1. Justice Douglas, *Zorach v. Clauson*, 343 U.S. 306, p. 313, 72 S.Ct. 679, p. 684, 96 L.Ed. 954 (1952).
2. David Barton, *America: Lessons From Nehemiah* (audiocassette), as quoted in a Christian Heritage class taught by Gene Hollick at Fountain of Life Church, Middletown, Pennsylvania, 2001.
3. "Mrs. Murray's War on God," by Robert Liston, *Saturday Evening Post,* July 24-August 1, 1964, p. 86.
4. "The Return of the Beatles," by Alfred G. Aronowitz, *Saturday Evening Post,* August 8-15, 1964, p. 28.
5. "Comment on Jesus Spurs A Radio Ban Against the Beatles," (AP) *New York Times,* August 5, 1966, p. 20; *Newsweek,* March 21, 1966, p. 52.

6. Harvey Day, *The Occult Illustrated Dictionary*, (Oxford University Press, 1976)

7. *Hit Parade Magazine*, October 1967, p. 14.

8. "An Infinity of Jimis," Interview by Robin Richman, *Life Magazine*, October 3, 1969, p. 74.

9. John Lennon, "Imagine" on album *Imagine* (1971).

10. Bart Millard, "I Can Only Imagine" on album *Almost There* performed by MercyMe. Copyright © 1999 Simpleville Music. Used by permission.

PART I

The Charge

Chapter 1

The Charge

This charge I commit to you, son Timothy, according to the prophecies previously made concerning you, that by them you may wage the good warfare. 1 Timothy 1:18

CHARGE: Greek = *paraggelia*, a mandate:—charge, command.[1]

Did you ever wish you had a mentor like Timothy had? Did you ever notice that in the opening chapter of the first letter Paul wrote to Timothy he gave him a charge, and he spoke to him about warfare? Paul was not playing a game. This was serious business. Paul was a man of God. Timothy was a man of God. And Paul, when writing by the Holy Spirit to his son in the faith, was by no means "wishy-washy." He did not ask Timothy to consider the things he wrote; rather, the apostle *commanded* him to carry out these things as a good soldier of Jesus Christ.

Just take a look at the *charges* Paul gave.

Paul's Charge to Timothy

All in all, the word *charge* can be found a total of 18 times in the New Testament Scriptures in the King James Version of the Bible. The apostle Paul used the word *charge* a total of five times when writing his first letter to Timothy.

The first time he used the word was when he wrote, *"...that thou mightest charge some that they teach no other doctrine"* (1 Timothy 1:3 KJV). The second time the word *charge* appears is when Paul wrote, *"This charge I commit unto thee, son Timothy, according to the prophecies which went before on thee, that thou by them mightest war a good warfare; holding faith, and a good conscience..."* (1 Timothy 1:18-19 KJV).

Paul also used it in giving a *charge* to the widows in the church to be blameless (1 Timothy 5:3-7). Again he told Timothy, *"I give thee charge in the sight of God, who quickeneth all things, and before Christ Jesus...that thou keep this commandment without spot, unrebukeable, until the appearing of our Lord Jesus Christ"* (1 Timothy 6:13-14 KJV).

And lastly, when speaking concerning the rich in the church, he wrote, *"Charge them that are rich in this world, that they be not highminded, nor trust in uncertain riches, but in the living God, who giveth us richly all things to enjoy"* (1 Timothy 6:17 KJV).

Paul had to be strong when dealing with the doctrines according to Christ. He had to be firm when addressing the widows or the rich. In the same way, Paul did not give Timothy the option of going some other way. He *charged* him to *"keep this commandment without spot, unrebukeable, until the appearing of our Lord."*

Are you *sure* you would like to have Paul for a mentor?

Paul wrote as a general would write to his lieutenant or captain. He wrote expecting Timothy to stand up and be the man of God that he was. God wants us as believers to be mature men of God as well. It is time for men of God to be the leaders that God has called them to be. It is time for the saints of God to be people who stand up and be counted. Christian recording artist Carmen said it like this in one of his songs: "Wimpy saints won't survive."

God's Charge to Joshua

In Joshua 1:6, when Joshua was preparing to lead the children of Israel into the Promised Land, the Lord told him, *"Be strong and of good courage."* Then again in verse 7 He said, *"Only be strong and very courageous."* Only two verses later He repeats, *"Have I not commanded you? Be strong and of good courage; do not be afraid, nor be dismayed, for the LORD your God is with you wherever you go"* (Joshua 1:9).

The Lord gave Joshua a *command* or a *charge* to *"be strong and of good courage."* Then, in verse 10, we see that Joshua *commanded* the officers, and in verse 11 the officers *commanded* the people. The people responded by saying, *"All that you* ***command*** *us we will do, and wherever you send us we will go. Just as we heeded Moses in all things, so we will heed you. Only the LORD your God be with you, as He was with Moses"* (Joshua 1:16-17).

Joshua was a type of Jesus. Just as Joshua led the children of Israel into Canaan, so Jesus is leading us into the Promised Land. In fact, the name *Joshua* means "The Lord saves" or "May the Lord save."

When we look at the Lord's words to Joshua, we see that He was not suggesting that Joshua do these things; He was *commanding* him to do be strong and of good courage. There are no options to obeying commands; you simply do them. God did not give Israel the "Ten Suggestions" or any other suggestions. He always gives His people commands to live by.

After all the commands had been spoken, the people responded to Joshua by saying this:

> *Whoever rebels against your command and does not heed your words, in all that you command him, shall be put to death. Only be strong and of good courage.* Joshua 1:18

I wonder how many people would come to our churches today if everyone who rebelled against the commands given through our spiritual leaders were put to death? In this age of grace that we the church are living in, we are not to kill the rebellious; but we are not to follow them either. Instead, we must deal with them according to God's Word. Otherwise they will stop us from fully experiencing God's promises.

Under Joshua's leadership the nation of Israel went into their Promised Land as an army. Today God wants us to be a *"holy nation"* (1 Peter 2:9) to go in and possess our Promised Land. He wants us to be those who not only hear but also obey His commands! We all must be strong and of good courage. We all must go forward in the whole armor of God. All of us need to obey and see to it that the "charge" given to us by the Word of God is heeded and carried out.

We know how to scream and holler out "Charge!" at a baseball game. We know how to use a "charge" card when making purchases. Now it is time for God's people to hear and heed His "charge."

Will you be one who follows this charge...in this generation?

Endnote

1. James Strong, *Strong's Exhaustive Concordance of the Bible* (Nashville, Tennessee: Holman Bible Publishers, n.d.), #G3852.

Chapter 2

This Charge I Commit to You..."First of All"

Therefore I exhort ***first of all*** *that supplications, prayers, intercessions, and giving of thanks be made for all men, for kings and all who are in authority, that we may lead a quiet and peaceable life in all godliness and reverence. For this is good and acceptable in the sight of God our Savior, who desires all men to be saved and to come to the knowledge of the truth. For there is one God and one Mediator between God and men, the Man Christ Jesus, who gave Himself a ransom for all, to be testified in due time.*
1 Timothy 2:1-6

These few lines are just a small portion of the words the apostle Paul wrote down and sent in a letter to Timothy, who at that time was a young pastor at the church at Ephesus around A.D. 62.

The Nelson Study Bible (New King James Version), when speaking of the relationship between Paul and Timothy and of the first book of Timothy, has this to say:

> *Timothy had accompanied Paul for years (Acts 16:1-3; 17:10; 20:4),assisting him and acting as his liaison to a number of churches. Paul had not only taught Timothy the essentials of the Christian faith, he had modeled Christian Leadership to him. Now Paul was leaving Timothy in charge of the church at Ephesus. From Macedonia, Paul wrote to encourage his "son" in the faith. In effect, this letter is Timothy's commission, his orders from his concerned teacher, the apostle Paul.*[1]

Before we take an in-depth look at the passage we quoted from 1 Timothy 2 at the beginning of this chapter, we need to back up a few verses and look at the preface or beginning of what Paul, by the Holy Ghost, was saying.

> *This charge I commit to you, son Timothy, according to the prophecies previously made concerning you, that by them you may wage the good warfare, having faith and a good conscience, which some having rejected, concerning the faith have suffered shipwreck, of whom are Hymenaeus and Alexander, whom I delivered to Satan that they may learn not to blaspheme.* 1 Timothy 1:18-20

Paul used the word *charge,* which is the Greek word *parangelia*, meaning "a proclamation, a command or commandment, [which] is strictly used of commands received from a superior and transmitted to others."[2]

Paul, Timothy and you and I are involved in a warfare, and as verse 18 says, we should be waging a *good* warfare. Later in the same letter the Holy Spirit tells us to *"fight the good fight of faith"* (1 Timothy 6:12). Again in 2 Timothy 2:3, the Word of God tells us to *"endure hardship as a good soldier of Jesus Christ."*

For many, many years the Christian church has failed to wage a "good" warfare or fight of faith. We have failed at being "good" soldiers of Jesus Christ. Why? Because this charge or command given by Paul was not just to one man,

Timothy; rather, it was given to all Christians who would read it and accept it as the Lord's Word to them.

Did you know that the Bible is God's written Word and that the New Testament is God's written Word to both Jew and Gentile—to all who believe that what it says is true? (See 2 Timothy 3:14-17.) So when we start reading 1 Timothy 2, the first thing we are told to do in carrying out the Holy Spirit's *charge* or command while waging a good warfare is *"that supplications, prayers, intercessions, and giving of thanks be made...."*

Now if that had been the whole of the "charge," I believe the church would be doing a pretty good job of what the Lord wants us to do. However, that is not the end of the story. You see, if the choice was left totally up to us—if we could pick and choose the people we bring before God in our time of prayer and giving of thanks—we would probably only pick the people we like on this planet. But the choice is not up to us. The Scripture says we are to pray

"...for all men..."

Not just your or my favorites, and

"...for kings..."

Not just the ones I like the best (notice the plurality), and for

"...all who are in authority..."

Not just the good ones (the ones I voted for) as opposed to the bad ones.

Have you ever heard the saying, "All means all and that's all all means"? Have you heard that God's ways are higher than our ways? I have learned over the years that there is a right way and a wrong way to do things, and in this case the right way—God's way—is not necessarily the way we've been used to doing it.

"Us Four and No More"

Christians have become very selfish and self-centered over the years. It seems that we have done all we can to make sure that we are well taken care of by God, searching out and praying His promises found in His Word and bringing before Him those things that concern ourselves.

God forgive me for the times that I prayed and gave thanks to Him for myself, my wife and my two daughters only. As the cliché goes, "God bless us four and no more." I don't pray that way anymore—I have repented.

The church, the body of Christ, has traveled far from this charge that God Himself instructed us to do *"first of all."* Throughout the ages the church has bad-mouthed, slandered, condemned and many times even murdered people who didn't measure up to our standards or who didn't do things the way we thought they should be done.

It is not our ways that matter, but God's. So before going any further in this, here is a breakdown of the four things Paul told Timothy that we need to be making to God. Included are the definition from *Strong's Concordance*, the English words used in the King James Bible the way they are translated from the Greek text, and some information quoted from the Nelson Study Bible in reference to 1 Timothy 2:1.

1. **Supplications:** (Greek: *deesis*). "A petition:—prayer, request, supplication."[3] This word "emphasizes personal need. The verb from which the noun is derived has the idea of 'petition.'"[4]

2. **Prayers:** (Greek: *prosevche*). "Prayer (worship); by impl. an oratory (chapel);—pray earnestly, prayer."[5] This word "is the general word for prayer. The term is always directed toward God with reverence or worship."[6]

3. **Intercessions:** (Greek *enteuxis*). "An interview, i.e. (spec.) supplication:—intercession, prayer."[7] This word "means 'approaching with confidence,' suggesting free access to God.[8]

4. **(Giving of) Thanks:** (Greek: *eucharistia*). "Gratitude; act. grateful language (to God, as an act of worship):—thankfulness, (giving of) thanks (-giving)."[9] This "is an attitude of gratitude, the act of praising God for what He has done for us."[10]

Our Four Part Strategy

Paul told the Christians at Thessalonica to *"pray without ceasing"* (1 Thessalonians 5:17). He also told the Christians at Ephesus to be *"praying always with all prayer and supplication"* (Ephesians 6:18). So as Christians, you and I should always be praying as we go throughout our day.

I believe that with *supplications* we are simply bringing our petitions or requests to God. These can be written down at times and can even appear in our church bulletins or ministry newsletters. They are needs that we can present to God as individuals or corporately in a local body of believers or even in larger group gatherings such as conventions, conferences or seminars.

I believe that the word *prayers* used here in verse 1, as the *Strong's Concordance* definition points out, is prayer that is spoken to God in a time of worship. Again, this can be done in an individual way or done in a time of corporate worship with other believers.

The third thing mentioned here is *intercessions*, which is when we make intercession for someone other than ourselves. I believe the most effective way to do this is by praying in the Spirit (Ephesians 6:18). The Scripture in Romans 8:26-27 says,

> *The Spirit* [Holy Spirit] *also helps in our weaknesses. For we do not know what we should pray for as we ought, but the Spirit Himself makes intercession for us with groanings which cannot be uttered. Now He who searches the hearts knows what the mind of the Spirit is, because He makes intercession for the saints according to the will of God.*

This is when we pray with, in or together with the Holy Spirit Himself. This is when we get beyond what we can come up with in our own thinking, especially when, as the Word of God says, *"we do not know what we should pray for as we ought."* The Holy Spirit knows the most effective way for you and I to be praying. He *"searches the hearts"*; He *"knows what the mind of the Spirit is"*; He *"makes intercession for the saints according to the will of God."* So then intercession is when we intercede or go before God on behalf of someone or something. (We will look at this more in Chapter 5.)

The last thing mentioned in the "first of all" charge is the *giving of thanks*. We are to be giving thanks to God for *"all men, for kings and all who are in authority"* in our times of prayer and worship. We are not supposed to be complaining about these people; rather, we are to be thanking God for all of them.

It is easy to thank God for the ones we are happy about, but the Lord wants us to get beyond our ways and pursue doing things His way.

It isn't easy to give thanks to God for the people who are not doing things in ways that please us. When was the last time you thanked God for that mean boss you have? Or for your employee who just screwed things up again? Or the driver who about ran you off the highway today? Or the senator who just introduced some legislation you didn't like? Or the president you think is doing such a lousy job? The list could go on and on.

Have you noticed that Christians can be some of the meanest creatures living here in this world? That is not God's will at all. God's strategy is for us to make supplications, prayers, intercessions and giving of thanks for *all* men. Did you notice that God's Word does not give room for exceptions? He could have told us to just do these four things when these folks are doing everything A-okay. He could have told us that this charge applies only to born-again applicants. Read that verse again if you need to. He did indeed say for *all* men, for kings, and for *all* in authority.

God Wants Us to Know Him

We could do a whole lot more discussion about this, but the bottom line is that this is God's way of doing things. Over the last two millenniums the church many times has failed to do things the way God intended for us to do them. God wants us to do things according to His plans, not according to our human nature.

It's time to change. It's time to wage a good warfare. Could this be a generation that will do His commandments, or as Paul expressed it to Timothy, His charges?

> *Now by this we know that we know Him, if we keep His commandments. He who says, "I know Him," and does not keep His commandments, is a liar, and the truth is not in him. But whoever keeps His word, truly the love of God is perfected in him. By this we know that we are in Him. He who says he abides in Him ought himself also to walk just as He walked.*
> 1 John 2:3-6

According to these verses, the way that we know that we know Jesus is by keeping His commandments. And when we keep His Word, the love of God is perfected in us, and that is how we know that we are in Him.

Do you "know that you know" Him? Are you keeping His commandments? Are you walking even as Jesus walked? Is the love of God being perfected in you?

This is God's will for His church in this generation, that we would know Him; that we would keep His commandments; that we would keep His Word; that His love would be perfected in us; that we would know that we are in Him and that we would walk even as He, Jesus, walked.

Could this be a generation that brings about change? Let's move forward; let's fight the *good* fight of faith. Let us be the *good* soldiers of Jesus Christ who are doing *good* warfare.

Can we be the ones who do things God's way? What are *you* going to do in this generation?

Endnotes

1. Earl D. Radmacher, gen. ed., *Nelson Study Bible*, New King James Version (Nashville, Tennessee: Thomas Nelson Publishers, 1997), p. 2039.
2. W.E. Vine, *Vine's Expository* Dictionary (Nashville, Tennessee: Thomas Nelson, Inc., 1977), p. 173.
3. James Strong, *Strong's Exhaustive Concordance of the Bible* (Nashville, Tennessee: Holman Bible Publishers, n.d.), #G1162.
4. Radmacher, *Nelson Study Bible*, p. 2043.
5. *Strong's Exhaustive Concordance*, #G4335.
6. Radmacher, *Nelson Study Bible*, p. 2043.
7. *Strong's Exhaustive Concordance*, #G1783.
8. Radmacher, *Nelson Study Bible*, p. 2043.
9. *Strong's Exhaustive Concordance*, #G2169.
10. Radmacher, *Nelson Study Bible*, p. 2043.

Chapter 3

Benefits of Carrying Out This Charge

You and I have been given a charge to keep and to carry out in this generation. When our Father gives us commands they are not only for His benefit, they are for our benefit as well. Our Commander and Chief, our Heavenly Father, loves us and like any good father He wants what is best for His children, and He always equips us with all that we need in order to do what He asks of us. If we will heed and obey God's charge, we will be rewarded.

A Quiet and Peaceable Life

Let's look at 1 Timothy 2:2b in a couple of different versions or translations of the Bible.

> *That we may lead a **quiet and peaceable life** in all godliness and honesty.* (King James Version)

That we may lead a ***quiet and peaceable life*** *in all godliness and reverence.* (New King James Version)

So that we may lead a ***tranquil and quiet life*** *in all godliness and dignity.* (New American Standard Version)

So that we can have ***quiet and peaceful lives*** *full of worship and respect for God.* (New Century Version)

In order that a ***tranquil and quiet life*** *we may lead in all piety and gravity.* (The Interlinear Greek-English New Testament)

According to the Word of God, if we will simply obey the charge written here in 1 Timothy 2:1-2 by the apostle Paul to offer *"supplications, prayers, intercessions, and giving of thanks...for all men, for kings and all who are in authority,"* then we will receive a life that is quiet and peaceable. No matter what translation or version of the Bible you normally use, you can see that the results are the same. If we, the church, will do what God asks of us, then He will see to it that we will enjoy lives that are peaceful and quiet in *all* godliness and reverence.

When I study the Bible, I like to look at the different translations to see how they compare. My favorite study Bible is a parallel Bible, called *The Contemporary Parallel New Testament*, which shows eight different translations side by side. The translations quoted above are some of them.

The last reference is from *The Interlinear Greek-English New Testament*, which translates the Greek text word by word over into English word by word. It is one of my favorite translations, and although it isn't easy reading, it is very accurate in its presentation of the New Testament Scriptures. In 1 Timothy 2:2b it says that our lives will be *"tranquil and quiet."*

Is your life tranquil or peaceful? How about quiet?

Strong's Exhaustive Concordance says that the word *peaceable* means "keeping one's seat (sedentary), i.e. (by impl.) still (undisturbed, undisturbing):—peaceable, quiet."[1] And of the word *quiet* it says, "(through the idea of stillness); tranquil:—quiet."[2]

Strong's definition of peaceable brings out the idea of keeping your seat, or being sedentary. *Webster's New World Dictionary* defines sedentary as "marked by much sitting."[3] *The Oxford American Dictionary* defines sedentary as "spending much time seated; requiring much sitting."[4] Have you been keeping your seat or are you constantly up and running?

It is God's will for us to have lives that are tranquil (peaceful, quiet, sedentary, etc.), not lives in which we need Tranquil™ to sleep at night. Didn't Jesus Himself say, *"Come to Me, all you who labor and are heavy laden, and I will give you rest. Take My yoke upon you and learn from Me, for I am gentle and lowly in heart, and you will find rest for your souls. For My yoke is easy and My burden is light"* (Matthew 11:28-30)?

Jesus will give you rest, and with it rest for your souls. Are you learning from Him?

Godliness and Reverence

Along with peace and quietness, God wants us to have *all* godliness and reverence. Paul was not speaking of the afterlife here. This is not the sweet by-and-by, but the today of our life, the here and now. Here again the word *all* is used. God wants us to have *all* that He has provided for us through Jesus.

Another similar passage is 2 Peter 1:2-4, where it says this about Jesus our Lord:

> *Grace and peace be multiplied to you in the knowledge of God and of Jesus our Lord, as His divine power has given to us all things that pertain to life and godliness, through the knowledge of Him who called us by glory and virtue, by which have been given to us exceedingly great and precious promises, that through these you may be partakers of the divine nature, having escaped the corruption that is in the world through lust.*

Even though we live in a corrupt world, God desires for us to be *"partakers of the divine nature."* He has given to us *"**great** and **precious** promises"* and *"**all** things that pertain to life and godliness."* It is God's will for us to be able to worship and serve Him now in this world and to live out lives that are at peace.

Good and Acceptable in God's Eyes

For this is good and acceptable in the sight of God our Savior. 1 Timothy 2:3

According to this verse, it is both *good* and *acceptable* in God's plan for us to have quiet and peaceable lives. I am going to get ahead of myself here, but I want to point out right now that it is not God's will for His people to live lives that are full of torment, depression, stress, unhappiness, restlessness and despair. If you have been told that God sent those things, in whatever way, shape or form, then you have been lied to! Torment and destruction are definitely *not* part of God's plan for you.

Paul, by the Holy Spirit, told us, *"Do not be conformed to this world, but be transformed by the renewing of your mind, that you may prove what is that good and acceptable and perfect will of God"* (Romans 12:2). Are you proving what is that good and acceptable and perfect will of God?

It is time for Christians to renew their minds to the truth that is found in God's Word. The only way for us to do that is to find out what the Scriptures have to say about everyday circumstances and situations that we live in. The apostle James put it this way: *"Receive with meekness the implanted word, which is able to save your souls"* (James 1:21).

We all need to have our souls saved from bad theology, bad doctrine and, simply put, flat-out lies that have infiltrated our beliefs about God.

Jesus said, *"The thief does not come except to steal, and to kill, and to destroy. I have come that they may have life, and that they may have it more abundantly. I am the **good** shepherd. The **good** shepherd gives His life for the sheep"* (John 10:10-11). One of the very first things we learn about the Lord is found in Psalm 23: The Lord is our Shepherd. Here in John 10 we see that not only is He our Shepherd, but He is our *Good* Shepherd as well.

If you are at a place where you feel like your life has been taken away from you or even destroyed, I want to tell you that God did not cause your trouble. The thief did! Who is the thief? Satan is the ultimate thief. He, in most cases, uses men and women to carry out his schemes and plans to take away all the things that God the Good Shepherd is providing for you in order for you to have life and have it more abundantly. Satan is not God. He is not omnipresent; he is only one individual being created by God Himself. Satan was the one who rebelled against God. His was the original sin; it wasn't what Adam and Eve did in the Garden. He is the thief, and he does not want you to know that God is good. He wants you to think that God is against you and that God is your problem. Satan is such a liar!

I hope you have noticed the word *good* appearing over and over in these pages. We see from these scripture passages and will continue to see as we go on that God is good and His plan or will for us is good. You and I must know this truth!

Here is a summary of the word *good* that we have seen so far in the Scriptures:

- 1 Timothy 1:18, concerning spiritual warfare: *"wage the good warfare."*
- 1 Timothy 2:3, concerning a quiet and peaceable life: *"for this is good and acceptable."*
- 2 Timothy 2:3, concerning being a soldier: *"as a good soldier of Jesus Christ."*
- Romans 12:2, concerning God's will: *"that good and acceptable and perfect will of God."*
- John 10:11, concerning the Lord: *"I am the good shepherd."*

Following are two more important pieces of evidence found in the Word of God relating to God's concern for you that I want you to see:

> *What shall we then say to these things? If God be for us, who can be against us? He that spared not his own Son, but delivered him up for us all, how shall he not with him also freely give us all things? Who shall lay any thing to the charge of God's elect? It is God that justifieth. Who is he that condemneth? It is Christ that died, yea rather, that is risen again, who is even at the right hand of God, who also maketh intercession for us. Who shall separate us from the love of Christ? shall tribulation, or distress, or persecution, or famine, or nakedness, or peril, or sword? As it is writ-*

ten, For thy sake we are killed all the day long; we are accounted as sheep for the slaughter. Nay, in all these things we are more than conquerors through him that loved us. For I am persuaded, that neither death, nor life, nor angels, nor principalities, nor powers, nor things present, nor things to come, nor height, nor depth, nor any other creature, shall be able to separate us from the love of God, which is in Christ Jesus our Lord. Romans 8:31-39 KJV

For the eyes of the Lord are over the righteous, and his ears are open unto their prayers: but the face of the Lord is against them that do evil. 1 Peter 3:12 KJV

Can you see in these verses that no matter what you are facing right now, God is for you? He is observing our lives. He is against those who do evil. Can you say, "I am more than a conqueror through Him who loved me"? Can you say in agreement with the Lord, "I am persuaded that nothing—including all other creatures—shall be able to separate me from the love of God"? By the way, Satan is one of those "other creatures" included in this list of things trying to conquer us.

God is for us. God is for you! Don't allow anyone to take away this truth about His love for you. He does love you; He gave His best for you—He gave His Son!

All **Men Can Be Saved!**

Who will have all men to be saved, and to come unto the knowledge of the truth. 1 Timothy 2:4 KJV

This is the heart of the Gospel message. This is where the church needs to go in this generation. This is the purpose of the charge. The first church, or early church, born at Pentecost, had an understanding of this reality.

They knew this truth: God's will is for *all* men to be saved!

It is not God's will for anyone to go to Hell. God wants all people to be saved and escape Hell. The Word of God says that the Lord is *"not willing that any should perish but that all should come to repentance"* (2 Peter 3:9). The Word of God also says that *"the goodness of God leads you to repentance"* (Romans 2:4).

Before time as we know it began, God intended for mankind to hold a special place in His creation and to be in relationship with Himself. The psalmist David said this about it:

> *What is man that You are mindful of him, and the son of man that You visit him? For You have made him a little lower than the angels, and You have crowned him with glory and honor. You have made him to have dominion over the works of Your hands; You have put all things under his feet, all sheep and oxen—even the beasts of the field, the birds of the air, and the fish of the sea that pass through the paths of the seas.* Psalm 8:4-8

Have you ever stopped and thought about the fact that God created all of mankind—all those people in the past, present and future? He is the Creator. Revelation 4:11 says about Him, *"For You created all things, and by Your will they exist and were created."*

He does not want His creation—men, women, boys and girls—to end up in an eternal hell or eternal fire, separated from His love. Jesus said in Matthew 25:41 that the everlasting fire was *"prepared for the devil and his angels."*

I believe that before Satan's rebellion against God, Hell did not exist. But because Satan was able to lead a host of angels against God, God created or "prepared" Hell, as Jesus said, for them as a destination in their sentencing or judgment placed on them by Almighty God.

Unfortunately, many people will end up in Hell or eternal fire as well because they did not believe that Jesus is the way, the truth and the life (John 14:6). He is the door into Heaven (John 10:9). There is salvation in no other, *"for there is no other name under heaven given among men by which we must be saved"* (Acts 4:12). The answer to the question of "What must I do to be saved?" is simply this: *"Believe on the Lord Jesus Christ, and you will be saved, you and your household"* (Acts 16:31).

> *Who will have all men to be saved, and to come unto the knowledge of the truth.* 1 Timothy 2:4 KJV

No, you are not experiencing déjà vu. I just wanted you to see this verse one more time. The New King James Version of this verse reads like this: *"Who desires all men to be saved and to come to the knowledge of the truth."*

I am so thankful to God that He desired for me to be saved. I am so thankful to God that He desired for you to be saved. And I am so thankful to God that He desires everyone who presently is not saved, to be saved. He wants them to come to the knowledge of the truth. At the same time, how can they come to the knowledge of the truth except by the saints of God (us) making supplications, prayers, intercessions and giving of thanks for them as well as sharing the Gospel with them? We have a charge to fulfill!

There is not one person living on this planet excluded from God's desire for their salvation. He wants *"all men to be saved."* Perhaps a mental list is flashing through your mind right now that includes all those whom you think God does not intend to be saved. Maybe you are seeing the faces on God's Most Un-Wanted posters. However, if you search out the New Covenant Scriptures, you will find that very few end up in a place of no possible forgiveness or repentance for their souls. I have found only two different situations like this in the New Testament. They are as follows:

> *Therefore I say to you, every sin and blasphemy will be forgiven men, but the blasphemy against the Spirit will not be forgiven men. Anyone who speaks a word against the Son of Man, it will be forgiven him; but whoever speaks against the Holy Spirit, it will not be forgiven him, either in this age or in the age to come.* Matthew 12:31-32

> *For it is impossible for those who were once enlightened, and have tasted the heavenly gift, and have become partakers of the Holy Spirit, and have tasted the good word of God and the powers of the age to come, if they fall away, to renew them again to repentance, since they crucify again for themselves the Son of God, and put Him to an open shame.* Hebrews 6:4-6

According to these verses, there is no forgiveness for those who speak against and blaspheme the Holy Spirit of God and no repentance for those who tasted *"the good word of God and the powers of the age to come"* yet turned their backs on the truth. The New Living Translation words it like this: *"It is impossible to bring such people to repentance again because they are nailing the Son of God to the cross again by rejecting him, holding him up to public shame"* (Hebrews 6:6).

The Message Bible also phrases Hebrews 6:4-6 in a way easy to understand:

> *Once people have seen the light, gotten a taste of heaven and been part of the work of the Holy Spirit, once they've personally experienced the sheer goodness of God's Word and the powers breaking in on us—if then they turn their backs on it, washing their hands of the whole thing, well, they can't start over as if nothing happened. That's impossible. Why, they've re-crucified Jesus! They've repudiated him in public!*

I believe that since Jesus has gone to the cross, the only way someone can end up in a place where salvation is no longer available is to blaspheme against and continue to blaspheme against the Holy Spirit. I have found that the ones who fall into such a category do not have any desire to read the *good* Word of God, to go to any church or to hear about God or His Word. They are in a very dangerous place in the eyes of the Lord.

Take stock of your life right now. Are you enjoying the benefits described in this chapter? Is your life peaceable and tranquil, are you experiencing godliness and reverence—which is good and acceptable before God? Keep on reading, for you are to rise up in this generation and fulfill the charge!

Endnotes

1 James Strong, *Strong's Exhaustive Concordance of the Bible* (Nashville, Tennessee: Holman Bible Publishers, n.d.), #G2272.

2 Strong, *Strong's Exhaustive Concordance*, #G2263.

3 David B. Guralnik, ed, *Webster's New World Dictionary* (New York: Warner Books, 1979), p. 539

4 Frank R. Abate, ed, *Oxford American Dictionary* (New York: Oxford University Press, 1999)

PART II
For All Men

But I say to you who hear: Love your enemies, do good to those who hate you, bless those who curse you, and pray for those who spitefully use you. To him who strikes you on the one cheek, offer the other also. And from him who takes away your cloak, do not withhold your tunic either. Give to everyone who asks of you. And from him who takes away your goods do not ask them back. And just as you want men to do to you, you also do to them likewise. But if you love those who love you, what credit is that to you? For even sinners love those who love them. And if you do good to those who do good to you, what credit is that to you? For even sinners do the same. And if you lend to those from whom you hope to receive back, what credit is that to you? For even sinners lend to sinners to receive as much back. But love your enemies, do good, and lend, hoping for nothing in return; and your reward will be great, and you will be sons of the Most High. ***For He is kind to the unthankful and evil.*** *Therefore be merciful, just as your Father also is merciful. Judge not, and you shall not be judged. Condemn not, and you shall not be condemned. Forgive, and you will be forgiven. Give, and it will be given to you: good measure, pressed down, shaken together, and running over will be put into your bosom. For with the same measure that you use, it will be measured back to you.*

Luke 6:27-38

Chapter 4

A Generation That Does Not Wrestle Against Flesh and Blood

Finally, my brethren, be strong in the Lord and in the power of His might. Put on the whole armor of God, that you may be able to stand against the wiles of the devil. For we do not wrestle against flesh and blood, but against principalities, against powers, against the rulers of the darkness of this age, against spiritual hosts of wickedness in the heavenly places. Therefore take up the whole armor of God, that you may be able to withstand in the evil day, and having done all, to stand. Stand therefore, having girded your waist with truth, having put on the breastplate of righteousness, and having shod your feet with the preparation of the gospel of peace; above all, taking the shield of faith with which you will be able to quench all the fiery darts of the wicked one. And take the helmet of salvation, and the sword of the

Spirit, which is the word of God; praying always with all prayer and supplication in the Spirit, being watchful to this end with all perseverance and supplication for all the saints—and for me, that utterance may be given to me, that I may open my mouth boldly to make known the mystery of the gospel, for which I am an ambassador in chains; that in it I may speak boldly, as I ought to speak. Ephesians 6:10-20

"Put on the whole armor of God." The Word of God, here again written by the hand of the apostle Paul and inspired by the Holy Spirit, has just issued another command to the body of Christ. Paul addressed *"the brethren,"* not just pastors or full-time ministers. Every single one of us in the church of Jesus Christ is included.

In fact, this was the final instruction that Paul, like a general, was giving to his fellow soldiers as he closed his letter to the church at Ephesus.

He wasn't recommending that they do these things. He wasn't suggesting that they do them. In fact, Paul didn't *ask* them to do this or even ask them to consider it. He *told* them to *"be strong in the Lord and in the power of His might"* and to *"put on the whole armor of God."* He didn't leave room for questions or comments. It was "Just do this so you can stand against the wiles or *schemings* of the devil."

Brothers and sisters, these words were written to you. Notice how the Holy Spirit used the words *you* and *your* in these verses. As a good soldier of Jesus Christ, *you* must be strong in the Lord. *You* must be strong in the power of His might. *You* must put on the whole armor of God to be able to stand. Unfortunately, many Christians are not putting on this armor of God. Many are not aware that there even is an armor of God for them to put on. Unforunately, many others are deceived into believing that Satan doesn't exist. A number of clergy are deceived as well, not teaching and preaching the truth about the enemy of God. Many in the church don't speak of Satan because the clergy themselves do not believe in his existence.

The Word of God—which is the truth—says that in the last days *"evil men and impostors will grow worse and worse, deceiving and being deceived"* (2 Timothy 3:13).

I believe we are living in the last days—and God told us a long time ago that evil men and impostors would be on the increase. I really hate to break the news to you, but it is a fact that there are *impostors* and *evil men*—and some of them are *spiritual leaders* in churches throughout America (and the whole earth, as far as that goes) who are deceiving their followers or parishioners. Many are themselves deceived, thinking in their own minds that everything is okay with them and God.

I have found a total of 17 warnings in the New Testament Scriptures telling us not to be deceived by men who would come. If the pastor of the church you presently attend does not believe that you need to put on the armor of God because Satan is just someone's invention or maybe your own evil human nature or dark side, then it would be a good idea for you to find another place to worship and to hear the Word of the Lord.

Since there already are a number of good books and teachings on the armor of God available, I only want to bring out a few points concerning the subject that I believe the Lord requires of this generation.

Our Real Enemy

Before Paul described each part of the armor, he made this extremely important statement:

> *"For we do not wrestle against flesh and blood."* Ephesians 6:12a

Church, did you see this? Can you hear the Holy Spirit saying it even now?

Since the Dark Ages, churches, Christians and denominations of all types—Independents, Catholics, Protestants, etc.—have been wrestling against flesh and blood. We can see with our eyes, hear with our ears, feel with our touch, smell with our noses and taste with our tongues, but according to the Word we must somehow get beyond all these physical sensations and recognize that the *source* of our problems is not a human being. If we could look into the spirit world, we'd see that there is a whole list of troublemakers that are found only in the supernatural realm.

It is against these spiritual entities that Christians are to be fighting or wrestling!

- Principalities

- Powers
- The rulers of the darkness of this age
- Spiritual hosts of wickedness in heavenly places

These are the true rebels—fallen angels that rebelled against God and His authority.

You cannot see them with your natural eyes, but they are just as real as the air you can't see but keeps you alive as you breathe it in and out day after day.

These demonic spirits constantly are trying to destroy us. While God and His angels constantly are working to bring about His good will on this planet, Satan and his associates are trying to prevent it from coming to pass.

I am getting ahead of myself again, but know this: If you put on the whole armor of God, you will withstand even in the *"evil day"* and you will be able to quench *"all the fiery darts of the wicked one"* (Ephesians 6:13, 16). In other places in His Word, God makes these statements: He always leads us in triumph (2 Corinthians 2:14). We are strong, the Word of God abides in us and we have overcome the wicked one (1 John 2:14). Whatever is born of God overcomes the world. And the victory that has overcome the world is our faith (1 John 5:4). We are of God and have overcome the spirit of antichrist because He who is in us (Jesus) is greater (1 John 4:4).

With God on our side, we are "Destined to Win" as the old DeGarmo & Key song said!

The devil has tricked us Christians in America into believing that men and women are our problem. There have been and always will be many people—*"flesh and blood"*—who appear to be causing us trouble in this world. Sometimes even the ones we love, who usually love us back, can appear to be against us.

It is time for this generation to recognize that there are satanic principalities, powers, rulers of the darkness of this world and spiritual hosts of wickedness influencing, manipulating and controlling human beings. They are the ones who can cause even unsuspecting individuals to carry out their plans.

Now that we know who are our real enemy is, we must obey the Lord's Word! He tells us how to deal with Satan. *"Be sober, be vigilant; because your adversary the devil walks about like a roaring lion, seeking whom he may devour. Resist him, steadfast in the faith..."* (1 Peter 5:8-9). *"Therefore submit to God. Resist the devil and he will flee from you"* (James 4:7). *"Lest Satan should take advantage of us; for we are not ignorant of his devices"* (2 Corinthians 2:11).

We believers are to resist Satan. He is, as these verses describe, seeking whom he may devour. He is looking for a place where he can take advantage of us. We have to be always "armed and ready" against his wiles and schemes.

You Must Forgive

One of the ways that Satan tries to get into our lives to steal, kill and destroy is by getting us into a place of anger against one another. Did you know that uncontrolled anger can get you into a place of sin, which then opens a door for Satan to destroy you? The New Century Version of the Bible says this: *"When you are angry, do not sin, and be sure to stop being angry before the end of the day. Do not give the devil a way to defeat you"* (Ephesians 4:26-27). If we allow him to, Satan will make us sin against each other by getting us into anger and strife with each other. *"For where envying and strife is, there is confusion and every evil work"* (James 3:16 KJV).

We must recognize what is going on here. Flesh and blood is not our enemy. There is a dark force (and it is not Darth Vader!) at work in the spiritual realm. We must drive or cast it out and be reconciled to the people with whom we are in strife or anger. According to God's Word, forgiveness is so important to our well-being that we cannot let the sun go down upon our wrath. Don't let the day end with any unforgiveness in your heart toward anyone.

Jesus said that when we pray, we must forgive our trespassers (those who sin against us) just as God the Father forgives us of all our sins. In this passage in Matthew chapter 6, Jesus was teaching His disciples how to pray. Immediately after He said "Amen," He said, *"For if you forgive men their trespasses, your heavenly Father will also forgive you. But if you do not forgive men their trespasses, neither will your Father forgive your trespasses"* (Matthew 6:14-15).

If you have ever heard any teaching or preaching on having faith in God, or on prayer, then you have probably seen these words of Jesus in Mark 11:22-26:

> *Have faith in God. For assuredly, I say to you, whoever says to this mountain, "Be removed and be cast into the sea" and does not doubt in his heart, but believes that those things he says will be done, he will have whatever he says. Therefore I say to you, whatever things you ask when you pray, believe that you receive them, and you will have them. And whenever you stand praying, if you have anything against anyone, forgive him, that your Father in heaven may also forgive you your trespasses. But if you do not forgive, neither will your Father in heaven forgive your trespasses.*

Did you notice the last two verses? You can be praying and believing in God and using your faith in God to move mountains, but if you have *"anything against anyone"* (unforgiveness), God Himself cannot and will not forgive you. Unforgiveness will cut off the blessings of God in your life. Unforgiveness will always leave a door open for Satan to take advantage of you.

Once again, we are not wrestling against flesh and blood. It is not about the people who have hurt or offended us. That may not be how it looks to us in the natural realm, but men and women really are not the problem. Something else is at work here in the realm of the spirit. And because it is a spiritual issue, we must react with spiritual weapons. In short, we must choose to walk in love toward people. We must choose to forgive people. We must recognize that a spiritual enemy is at work and war against him.

Jesus, while hanging on the cross, set forth the example of choosing to forgive. This is what He said at His hour of death: *"Father, forgive them, for they do not know what they do"* (Luke 23:34.)

First John 5:18-19 says this:

> *We know that whoever is born of God does not sin; but he who has been born of God keeps himself, and the wicked one does not touch him. We know that we are of God, and the whole world lies under the sway of the wicked one.*

The Scriptures are clear on who the real enemy is. Yet, more often than not, the church has been tricked into thinking that men and women are the problem. It is time we comprehended who the real culprit is in the trouble we might be facing even now.

Do you remember reading of when Jesus turned to Peter and said to him, *"Get behind Me, Satan! You are an offense to Me, for you are not mindful of the things of God, but the things of men"* (Matthew 16:23)? Jesus knew that Peter was not the problem; it was Satan.

Satan had planted some ideas in Peter's thinking and used Peter to rebuke the Lord concerning Him going to Jerusalem to die for us and being raised again on the third day. Jesus did not rebuke Peter; instead, He recognized the devil behind the scenes and rebuked *him*. Just a few verses before this scene, Jesus had given Simon Bar-Jonah the new name of Peter and had given Peter and the other disciples the keys of the kingdom of heaven (see Matthew 16:17-19). Obviously Satan had been right there and had begun scheming to stop what God was doing in the lives of these men. Jesus had given them the authority to bind and loose in both the heavenly and earthly realms. So Satan immediately influenced Peter in an attempt to stop Jesus from completing His purpose for coming to earth, which was to go to the cross.

Jesus recognized that Satan was the one who needed to be rebuked. We too need to recognize that many times it is Satan or one of Satan's assistants behind the scenes of the problems we face. And we disarm him by walking in forgiveness and Christ-like love.

Now It Is Time

> *And do this, knowing the time, that now it is high time to awake out of sleep; for now our salvation is nearer than we first believed. The night is far spent, the day is at hand. Therefore let us cast off the works of darkness, and let us put on the armor of light. Let us walk properly, as in the day, not in revelry and drunkenness, not in lewdness and lust, not in strife and envy. But put on the Lord Jesus Christ, and make no provision for the flesh, to fulfill its lusts.* Romans 13:11-14

> *Do this because we live in an important time. It is now time for you to wake up from your sleep, because our salvation is nearer now than when*

we first believed. The "night" is almost finished, and the "day" is almost here. So we should stop doing things that belong to darkness and take up the weapons used for fighting in the light. Let us live in a right way, like people who belong to the day. We should not have wild parties or get drunk. There should be no sexual sins of any kind, no fighting or jealousy. But clothe yourselves with the Lord Jesus Christ and forget about satisfying your sinful self. Romans 13:11-14 (New Century Version)

It is *"high time"* for the saints of God (including you and I) to wake up and put on the armor of God, or *"armor of light"* as used here. If you have been waiting for God to put His armor on you, you'll wait forever. It just will never happen. Why? He has already given it to you. *You* have to put it on! I like how the New Century Version says to *"take up the weapons used for fighting in the light."* The day is at hand; we must put on the Lord Jesus Christ. We must stop living our lives to please our sinful desires. Christ is in us, *"the hope of glory"* (Colossians 1:27), and we must allow Him to use us in any and every way possible to bring about His will in this earth. God has told all of us to be strong in Him and to put on His armor: *"Be strong in the Lord and in the power of His might. Put on the whole armor of God, that you may be able to stand against the wiles of the devil"* (Ephesians 6:10-11).

Just as Joshua had to be strong and courageous, so we have to be strong in the Lord and in the power of His might. Did you notice the word *you* in Ephesians 6:11? When Paul instructed the church to put on the armor God, he used the word *you* three times, the word *your* two times and the word *we* one time. By this the Word of God is telling us what *we* must do to be overcomers against the powers of darkness. That means you and me! The Bible often uses the word *you* when speaking to the one who is hearing or reading it. When I read such passages, I see the Scriptures as speaking directly to me. Again, God's Word is not suggesting or even asking me to respond. It is telling me that this is what I must do to avoid getting wiped out by the satanic forces in this world.

Read this verse and make it personal: *"Take up the whole armor of God, that you* [insert your name] *may be able to withstand in the evil day, and having done all, to stand"* (Ephesians 6:13). This Scripture does not tell you to use some of the armor; it tells you to take up the *whole* armor of God. This is God's armor you are putting on so that you can withstand the enemy and his attacks against you in the evil day. Then God's Word says, *"having done all, to stand."* You can be victorious; you can be more than a conqueror, if you will just do what the Lord requires you to do.

According to what I see in Ephesians 6, it must be very dangerous to be in this world and not know about the armor of God, or to know about it and not use it in fighting the good fight of faith. In many cases, God's grace is there to help us win our battles in this life when we are not doing the things that He has instructed us to do. You could say that there are many spiritual "streakers" in the body of Christ—people who do not know how to put on and use the weapons of the armor of God. They're running around unclothed. God's grace is abundant for such, but it's time to change. If you know about the things we have been looking at in this chapter, then you are responsible along with me to help others in the body of Christ take up the whole armor of God as well. Just read 1 Thessalonians 5:14-15: *"Comfort the fainthearted, uphold the weak, be patient with all. See that no one renders evil for evil to anyone, but always pursue what is good both for yourselves and for all."*

Remember, this is a *good warfare* and we are *good soldiers* of Jesus Christ. Sadly, many casualties of war sit with us on Sunday mornings. It is part of our duty to comfort the fainthearted, uphold the weak and be patient with all. This can be hard to do, but we absolutely must help others who are hurting and needing someone to come alongside them and stand with them. We must help people to stand until they can stand on their own.

Chuck Girard, one of the pioneers of Jesus Rock music and a former member of the group called Love Song, released an album back in 1983 called *The Name Above All Names*. It had a song on it called "Don't Shoot the Wounded."[1] Just read some of the lyrics:

It's easy to love the people who are standing hard and fast,
pressing on to meet that higher calling.
But the ones who might be struggling, we tend to judge too harshly
and refuse to try and catch them when they're falling.

We put people into boxes and we draw our hard conclusions

and when they do the things we know they should not do

we sometimes write them off as hopeless and we throw them to the dogs.

Our compassion and forgiveness sometimes seems in short supply so I say....

DON'T SHOOT THE WOUNDED, THEY NEED US MORE THAN EVER.

THEY NEED OUR LOVE NO MATTER WHAT IT IS THEY'VE DONE.

SOMETIMES WE JUST CONDEMN THEM, AND DON'T TAKE TIME TO HEAR THEIR STORY.

DON'T SHOOT THE WOUNDED, SOMEDAY YOU MIGHT BE ONE.

The church of Jesus Christ has suffered war casualties and had many losses, but it is time to re-unite, re-focus, take up the shield of faith and quench all the fiery darts of the wicked one.

The Lord is coming back for a victorious church. The night truly is spent and the day is at hand. Can this be a generation that casts off the works of darkness in every area of life in every situation? Can this be a generation that puts on the armor of God and puts on the Lord Jesus Christ?

Can this be the generation that fulfills the charge?

Endnote

1. Chuck Girard, "Don't Shoot the Wounded." *Name Above All Names.* Sea of Glass Music, 1982. Used by permission.

Chapter 5

A Generation That Completes the Armor of God

(Praying in the Spirit for All the Saints)

Finally, my brethren, be strong in the Lord and in the power of His might. Put on the whole armor of God, that you may be able to stand against the wiles of the devil. For we do not wrestle against flesh and blood, but against principalities, against powers, against the rulers of the darkness of this age, against spiritual hosts of wickedness in the heavenly places. Therefore take up the whole armor of God, that you may be able to withstand in the evil day, and having done all, to stand. Stand therefore, having girded your waist with truth, having put on the breastplate of righteousness, and having shod your feet with the preparation of the gospel of peace; above all, taking the shield of faith with which you will be able to quench all the fiery darts of the wicked one. And take the helmet of salvation, and the sword of the Spirit, which is the word of God; praying always with all prayer and supplication in the

> *Spirit, being watchful to this end with all perseverance and supplication for all the saints.* Ephesians 6:10-18

After the apostle Paul wrote to the church at Ephesus about putting on the whole armor of God, he went on to show us in verse 18 how to *complete* the putting on of God's armor by *"praying always with all prayer and supplication in the Spirit."*

By now we have learned from Paul what the armor of God is and we have put it in place in our lives: truth, righteousness, the gospel of peace, faith, salvation, the Word of God.

Keep in mind that Satan, our enemy, does not want us to put on the whole armor of God. He does not want Christians to know that it even exists. Why? If he can keep the body of Christ in the dark about our spiritual weapons, then he can succeed against us in his schemes.

Although he succeeded during the Dark Ages, I am so thankful to God that today we can open up our Bibles and read for ourselves how to wage a good warfare! *"Lest Satan should take advantage of us; for we are not ignorant of his devices"* (2 Corinthians 2:11). *"Resist the devil and he will flee from you"* (James 4:7).

In fact, God *wants* you and I as His people to know His will—and He wants us to know it in *all* wisdom and spiritual understanding.

> *For this reason we also, since the day we heard it, do not cease to pray for you, and to ask that you may be filled with the knowledge of His will in all wisdom and spiritual understanding; that you may have a walk worthy of the Lord, fully pleasing Him, being fruitful in every good work and increasing in the knowledge of God; strengthened with all might, according to His glorious power, for all patience and longsuffering with joy; giving thanks to the Father who has qualified us to be partakers of the inheritance of the saints in the light.* Colossians 1:9-12

God is not holding anything back! He wants us to get *all* that is available to us through Jesus Christ. He didn't make provision for us to get just a little bit of the knowledge of His will; rather, He wants us to be filled with it. He wants us to be fully pleasing Him, not halfway pleasing Him. He wants us to be fruitful in *every* good work, strengthened with *all* might, having *all* patience and long-suffering with joy.

It is time that we accept what He has for us and begin to agree with God that these things are working in our lives, giving thanks to the Father, Who has "qualified us (King James Version says "made us") to be partakers of the inheritance of the saints." It is God's word that says this about us, so when Satan tries to bring you down, remember what God has said about you, and tell the devil that your Father has qualified you to be a partaker of the inheritance given to you in Christ Jesus!

Completing the Armor of God

God wants us to be *"filled with the knowledge of His will in all wisdom and spiritual understanding,"* as we have just seen. Concerning the armor of God, He wants us to put on all of it—the whole of it, not lacking any part. He wants us to get *all* of the wisdom and spiritual understanding concerning it as well. (Satan would rather we not know or put on any of it.) But when we do—when we put on and use to its fullest capacity each and every piece—then we –are fully dressed soldiers warring against the principalities, the powers, the rulers of the darkness and the spiritual hosts of wickedness in the high or heavenly places.

So after Paul has instructed the church about the armor and its pieces, he then went on to say, *"Praying always with all prayer and supplication in the Spirit, being watchful to this end with all perseverance and supplication for all the saints"* (Ephesians 6:18).

This is what we are to do after putting on the whole armor of God. This is how we complete the purpose of it! This is once again the charge given to the church "first of all" put into action. Do you see it? We are to be *"praying **always** with all prayer and supplication in the Spirit...with all perseverance and supplication for all the saints."* Doesn't this sound like, *"I exhort first of all that supplications, prayers, intercessions, and giving of thanks be made for all men"*?

In the Spirit

The only biblical way we are going to be successful in completing our charge *first of all* is by doing it according to the Word of God—and Ephesians 6:18 says to make prayer and supplication in the Spirit.

The phrase *in the Spirit* here is speaking of the Holy Spirit using us to bring forth prayers and supplications to God by His ability working in and through us. We are to be praying "in the Spirit"; this is when our spirits and the Holy Spirit in us pray. When the apostle Paul wrote this, he wanted us to know that the Holy Spirit needs to be involved in our praying and making supplications.

Paul wrote this in 1 Corinthians 14:14-15 concerning prayer:

> *For if I pray in a tongue, my spirit prays, but my understanding is unfruitful. What is the conclusion then? I will pray with the spirit, and I will also pray with the understanding. I will sing with the spirit, and I will also sing with the understanding.*

In verse 14 Paul said that when he prays in a tongue, *his spirit prays*. Then in verse 15 he said he would pray *"with the spirit."* That is not the same as praying with the understanding. When you or I, like Paul, pray in or with the spirit, our understanding is unfruitful. Our mind does not know what is being said. Look at 1 Corinthians 14:2:

> *For he who speaks in a tongue does not speak to men but to God, for no one understands him; however, in the spirit he speaks mysteries.*

In other words, when someone speaks in a tongue, no one understands what is being said except for God Himself. *"In the spirit"* he is speaking mysteries!

When a Christian man, woman, boy or girl prays in the spirit, he or she is allowing the Holy Spirit of God to bring forth words from the inner being where the Holy Spirit abides (John 14:17). Then, as Romans 8:26 says,

> *Likewise the Spirit also helps in our weaknesses. For we do not know what we should pray for as we ought, but the Spirit Himself makes intercession for us with groanings which cannot be uttered.*

When we do not know what we should pray for, the Holy Spirit does—and He wants us to allow Him to help us in our weaknesses. He wants us to let Him help us pray. We do that by praying in the spirit.

It all began in the book of Acts. The Scriptures say that when the Day of Pentecost had fully come, the Holy Spirit was poured out on all flesh just as the prophet Joel had prophesied hundreds of years before—and the disciples of Jesus *"began to speak with other tongues, as the Spirit gave them utterance"* (Acts 2:4).

So, from what we can see in the Scriptures, *"praying always with all prayer and supplication in the Spirit"* refers to praying in a heavenly, Holy Spirit-given language called tongues.

Satan has fought and will continue to fight against Christians "speaking in tongues," "praying in tongues" and "singing in tongues." Why? One reason is that he absolutely cannot tell what a saint of God is talking to Almighty God about when he or she is praying in tongues because it is a mystery that only God knows. No man or devil understands it unless God the Father, Jesus or the Holy Spirit reveals it.

Is it possible then that when we pray in tongues (or with a heavenly language) that God can, by the Holy Spirit, relay the interpretation back to the one praying or the one(s) being prayed for in a *rhema* (spoken) word? I believe that He can and does do so when we pray in the spirit.

Have you ever been in church when a "tongue" is spoken and then an "interpretation" given with it? These are gifts from God being manifested among the church (1 Corinthians 12).

This is an exciting time! God is manifesting His presence by speaking to us through the use of human mouths and human tongues. And He will continue to do so right up until Jesus Christ returns.

Perhaps God not only gives us the interpretation when we pray in tongues, but also takes those "mysteries" and makes their meanings known to the unseen forces or even the angels of God to cause them to obey His voice!

Being Watchful

The second half of Ephesians 6:18 instructs us on another aspect to completing our armor of God.

> *...Being watchful to this end with all perseverance and supplication for all saints.* Ephesians 6:18

The Greek word *agrupneo*, translated as "being watchful" in the New King James Version and as "watching" in the King James Version, is defined as, "To be sleepless...The word expresses not mere wakefulness, but the watchfulness of those who are intent upon a thing."[1]

Armored saints of God, those who are praying in the Spirit, we are to be *watchful* with all perseverance and supplication for all the saints.

It is our job, so to speak, to be watchful. As the army of God in the earth, collectively, we the church need to be in continual prayer, making supplications, intercessions and giving of thanks for all men.

The *good* soldiers of Jesus Christ are those who are watchful, who do not quit until the prayers made bring about results. Finis Dake, in his reference Bible, says that without being watchful, prayer and Christian armor are ineffectual.[2]

Jesus spoke of the importance of watching and praying for those who are living at the time of His Second Coming:

> *Take heed, watch and pray; for you do not know when the time is. It is like a man going to a far country, who left his house and gave authority to his servants, and to each his work, and commanded the doorkeeper to watch. Watch therefore, for you do not know when the master of the house is coming—in the evening, at midnight, at the crowing of the rooster, or in the morning—lest, coming suddenly, he find you sleeping. And what I say to you, I say to all: Watch!* Mark 13:33-37

> *But take heed to yourselves, lest your hearts be weighed down with carousing, drunkenness, and cares of this life, and that Day come on you unexpectedly. For it will come as a snare on all those who dwell on the face of the whole earth. Watch therefore, and pray always that you may be counted worthy to escape all these things that will come to pass, and to stand before the Son of Man.* Luke 21:34-36

Doesn't this sound a lot like Ephesians 6:18? I believe in this last century God Himself has used the fivefold gifts of apostles, pastors, teachers, prophets and evangelists (Ephesians 4:11) to equip the saints of God in the whole armor of God like no other time in the history of the church. In this century we have television, radio, audiotapes, videos, CDs, DVDs, books and millions of Bibles. In the days of the book of Acts and the early years of Christianity it would have been impossible to find out about the whole armor of God and how to use it effectively (as we do from Ephesians 6)—unless you could locate the apostle Paul or someone who had been with him.

Paul received divine revelations from the Lord Jesus Himself concerning the things that he wrote down in his letters to the churches (2 Corinthians 12:1). Satan did not want the body of Christ to know all the truth Jesus had given to Paul, which he was sharing with the saints of God, so Satan sent one of his agents to *"buffet"* him (2 Corinthians 12:7). The Greek word for "buffet" is *kolaphizo*, which means "to rap with the fist."[3] Satan did not and does not want us to know who we are in Christ! He tried his best to "beat" Paul. The good news is this: He didn't succeed! At the end of his life Paul said, *"I have fought the good fight, I have finished the race, I have kept the faith"* (2 Timothy 4:7). Satan did not beat Paul; rather, Paul, with the help of the Holy Spirit, beat Satan!

For two millenniums, even though he is in Heaven and far from Satan or any other demon, the apostle Paul continues to beat the devil whenever a believer decides that he too can be strong in the Lord and in the power of His might, puts on the whole armor of God so that he can stand against the wiles of the devil, and having done all, is still standing!

With All Perseverance and Supplication

There is a third part to completing the armor of God.

> *...with all perseverance and supplication for all the saints.* Ephesians 6:18

Being fully armored, praying always in the Spirit, being watchful—and now add to all of that *"with all perseverance."*

Perseverance is a word that no one likes, right? However, if you intend to be a successful soldier of Jesus Christ, you will have to persevere in prayers and supplications. There is no quitting allowed in the army in which God Himself has enlisted you. Victory always comes to those who after having done all, are still standing.

Did you know that the word *perseverance* is found only one time in the King James Version? That one time is right here in Ephesians 6:18. And the verb form of *persevere* is not used at all in the King James Version.

The Greek word for "perseverance" is *proskarteresis.* Its definition from *Vine's Expository Dictionary* is "to be steadfast...denotes to continue stedfastly in a thing and give unremitting care to it,"[4] and from *Dake's* is "to adhere firmly to. Be close in pursuit of; always intent upon your object in prayer."[5]

The Bible tells us only one thing we are to persevere in, and that is supplication for all saints. We already have looked at supplication being made in the charge given "first of all" in Chapter 2. However, let's look at Dake's definition. His *Annotated Reference Bible* says supplication is "an entreating; continued strong and incessant pleadings until the prayer is answered."[6] The Greek word is *deesis* and is translated as "request" or "supplication" as well as "prayer," 12 times in the King James Version. *This* is what we must persevere in as good soldiers of Jesus Christ!

For All Saints

> *...Being watchful to this end with all perseverance and supplication for all saints.* Ephesians 6:18

This is the grand finale of the whole matter at hand—the completing of the armor of God.

All that we do here with the armor and praying and making supplication, is to be done *for all saints.* Not just *by* all saints but *for* all of them.

Notice: it's not for "me, myself and I," but "they, themselves and them," the saints of God!

I believe that God has been equipping us individually, and now that we are prepared He is, in this generation, moving us into a place where the church collectively will fight a spiritual warfare! No longer will we take on all of the forces of darkness by ourselves, fighting the devil one on one, but we are joining forces to stop all of Satan's advancements against the church.

Have you heard that Jesus is coming back for a glorious church? Did you know that Paul talked about such a church right before he taught on the armor of God?

Ephesians 5:26-27 says, *"That He might sanctify and cleanse it* [speaking of the church] *with the washing of water by the word, that He* [Jesus] *might present it to Himself a glorious church, not having spot, or wrinkle, or any such thing; but that it should be holy and without blemish." (KJV)*

According to *Strong's Exhaustive Concordance*, the Greek word for "glorious" is *endoxos*, meaning "in glory, i.e. splendid, (fig.) noble"; it is translated as *glorious, gorgeous, gorgeously* and *honourable* in the King James Version.[7]

Jesus is coming back for a *glorious* church! Not a defeated church, not a backslidden church and not a selfish church. No, we are not going down in a blaze of glory! We are going *up* in a blaze of glory!

Don't ever let anyone convince you that the church is going to be all run down at the end of the age. That is a lie of the devil. God's word says that Jesus is going to present it to Himself as glorious!

I do not think it is a coincidence that the "glorious church" is one that puts on the whole armor of God and beats the devil every time. Church, we are to quench all—100 percent—of the fiery darts of the wicked one.

Neither is the glorious church an isolated group of people only concerned about themselves. A glorious church is not a group of people that have placed a man at the head. No, the glorious church has as its head Jesus Christ our Lord, and all of its members are not only interested in their part of the body, but also have a concern for the whole of the parts of the body, collectively and universally.

The apostle Paul wrote to the Colossians and warned, *"Let no one cheat you of your reward"*; they were to watch out for people who do not hold *"fast to the Head, from whom all the body, nourished and knit together by joints and ligaments, grows with the increase that is from God"* (Colossians 2:18-19). Saints of God, are you holding fast to the Head, Jesus Christ? Know the Head, love Him and hold fast to Him. Never let go of Him—He is *"the way, the truth, and the life"* (John 14:6). Anyone else claiming to be the head of the church is a fraud! If you are not sure that you are presently in the truth, I recommend you read 2 Peter chapter 2. In that chapter the Holy Spirit talks about false prophets and false teachers and those who deceive many.

Do you want to be a part of this glorious church that Jesus will present to Himself? A church that is strong in the Lord and in the power of His might? A church that is not getting all that they can for themselves, but rather going to war with and for the whole body of Christ on both a local and universal level?

This last-days, glorious church is one that armored soldiers are willing to pray for *"always with all prayer and supplication in the Spirit, being watchful to this end with all perseverance and supplication for all saints."*

The Bible does not say "the saints who are your buddies," or "the saints who are your relatives" or even "the saints in your local congregation." God wants us to go farther than that! He wants us to get beyond our natural knowledge and natural understanding and once again get over into that realm where He is—the realm of faith.

Praying for *all* saints might seem impossible to you, but it can be done. With God all things are possible, and by praying "in the Spirit," we can accomplish all things. We cannot carry out this duty in our own ability. It can be done only by praying and making supplication "in the Spirit." I am convinced that when we pray in the Spirit, we do not miss the will of God in our praying. The Holy Spirit is the Third Person of the Trinity; He is the one who is at work in and throughout the whole world. He works not only in and through you, but also in and through all the saints of God who live on planet Earth. He knows all and sees all concerning the church of Jesus Christ.

He knows how to pray when we don't know how to pray. He knows what is happening at this very moment in the lives of every member of the body of Christ, and He is ready and waiting for you and I to submit to Him and allow Him to use us to pray with His ability.

When we pray in the Spirit we don't pray ineffectively, missing the mark; instead, we hit the target right in the center of the bull's eye. When we yield our lives and our prayers to the Holy Spirit, there are no limits to what God can do "for all the saints." (Gender and age make no difference.)

At this very hour there could be a saint on the other side of the planet, a brother or a sister in the body of Christ, who needs immediate help. Could you be the one to pray in the Spirit to bring about salvation on behalf of this saint?

When I was in high school, I liked to lift weights. I usually did this alone in my parents' basement. Not the safest thing to do, I know. One summer evening when I was bench pressing around 170 pounds, my arms gave out and

I dropped the barbell set on my face. This was not a good thing! The weight came down on my nose and my whole face went numb. There was blood everywhere. Nevertheless, I managed to get myself upstairs to where my parents were. Our family physician was Jesus, so my parents "took" me to Him immediately.

Meanwhile, I found out later, one of my closest friends was at his own house minding his own business when the Holy Spirit interrupted him and told him that he needed to pray for me right then. My friend did what all of us typically do; he reasoned with himself, thinking, *Why do I need to pray for Joel? Joel is fine. What does he need prayer for?* But the Holy Spirit impressed on him an urgency that would not go away, so he began to pray in the Spirit for me. When we compared notes later, we discovered that he had been praying at exactly the hour that I was injured.

In the end I and my nose were both fine. I never did go to the hospital or any other doctor over that incident, and I went to work the next day, completely healed as far as I can remember. I know I didn't have a broken nose, though I should have from all that weight.

Thank God my friend obeyed and prayed in the Spirit for me!

God Speaks Through Us

In the Old Testament, God spoke to the prophets, priests and kings, and they wrote down what they heard. In the New Testament God spoke audibly at least two times—at Jesus' baptism and at the Mount of Transfiguration—but have you ever noticed how God spoke to His early church?

He spoke through men. Matthew, Mark, Luke, John, Paul, Peter, James and all the rest of the writers of the New Testament spoke or wrote down the Word of God as they were inspired by the Holy Spirit. God spoke through men and women by the Holy Spirit in them. God speaks the same way today. He is speaking, talking and praying through people who will allow Him to use the words of their mouths.

For example, take a typical Sunday morning in my church. During the whole time we are there worshiping and praising God and hearing the Word of God preached, not one time do I hear an audible voice from Heaven that I could recognize as the voice of Father God. But there are plenty of times throughout the service when I did hear the word or voice of God coming out of the mouths of people whom God is using, by the Holy Spirit, to speak through and minister to me.

On such a Sunday morning service God did not physically come to my church, stand behind the pulpit and preach to the congregation, and I can make a pretty good guess that He did not physically show up and preach at your church either. But He did in actuality show up and preach in our churches; He simply used the mouths of His servants to bring forth His Word. And if you will let Him, He will use you in the same way to speak or pray words that will bring about change as you make prayers and supplications in the Spirit.

Church, let's not quarrel about tongues or how to pray. Let's just pray. And when you pray, ask the Holy Spirit to use you to speak forth words that are empowered by Him. Ask Him to use you to bring about His will in the life of someone. Ask Him to use you to bring words of life to situations. The Word of God becomes the sword of the Spirit when the saints of God speak it forth. I believe that when we pray in the Spirit our words change into His words. They become a sword of the Spirit and accomplish what the Lord intends them to do in the realm of the Spirit!

Hebrews 4:12-13 says,

> *For the word of God is living and powerful, and sharper than any two-edged sword, piercing even to the division of soul and spirit, and of joints and marrow, and is a discerner of the thoughts and intents of the heart. And there is no creature hidden from His sight, but all things are naked and open to the eyes of Him to whom we must give account.*

The spoken Word of God affects the spirit, soul and body when it is brought forth out of the mouths of God's people.

It is time for the church to pray in the Spirit, involving the Spirit in our prayers, allowing the Holy Spirit of God to use us in our times of praying and making supplications for all saints. If you are born again and have been filled with the Holy Spirit, then He lives in you! First John 3:24 says, *"Now he who keeps His commandments abides in Him, and He in him. And by this we know that He abides in us, by the Spirit whom He has given us."*

Let the Spirit of God use you. Let Him speak through your lips, using your words spoken in prayer for all the saints.

Could this be what the apostle James was trying to tell us when he said, *"...pray for one another, that you may be healed. The effective, fervent prayer of a righteous man avails much"* (James 5:16)?

Will we be the generation that rises up to fulfill the charge?

Endnotes

1. W.E. Vine, *Vine's Expository Dictionary* (Nashville, Tennessee: Thomas Nelson Publishers, 1997), p. 1213.

2. Finis Jennings Dake, *Dake's Annotated Reference Bible*, Large Note Edition (Lawrenceville, Georgia: Dake Bible Sales, Inc., 1961, 1963, 1981), p. 212 NT.

3. James Strong, *Strong's Exhaustive Concordance of the Bible* (Nashville, Tennessee: Holman Bible Publishers, n.d.), #G2852.

4. Vine, *Vine's Expository Dictionary*, pp. 850, 79.

5. Dake, *Dake's Annotated Reference Bible*, p. 212 NT.

6. Dake, *Dake's Annotated Reference Bible*, p. 212 NT.

7. Strong, *Strong's Exhaustive Concordance*, #G1741.

Chapter 6

A Generation That Remembers the POWs in the Body

Let brotherly love continue. Hebrews 13:1

Remember the prisoners as if chained with them—those who are mistreated—since you yourselves are in the body also. Hebrews 13:3

We live in a "dog eat dog" world. In the 1970s a song played on the radio that pretty much summed up the ideology of that time, called "Looking Out for Number One." It told us to view ourselves as number one and to look out for ourselves only.

God has a different plan than that for us to live by. God—not us—is to be Number One in everything we do. Jesus said,

> *" 'You shall love the* LORD *your God with all your heart, with all your soul, and with all your mind.' This is the first and great commandment."* Matthew 22:37-38

He continued by saying,

> *"And the second is like it: 'You shall love your neighbor as yourself.'"* Matthew 22:39

The world says, "Love yourself." The Word says, "Love your neighbor as yourself." The apostle Paul, when writing to the Philippians, said this:

> *Let nothing be done through selfish ambition or conceit, but in lowliness of mind let each esteem others better than himself. Let each of you look out not only for his own interests, but also for the interests of others.* Philippians 2:3-4

Christians, we are to be looking out for Number Two—other people. Not to prevent them from getting our position, but rather to see to it that they are placed above even our thinking of ourselves. We are to *"esteem others better than"* ourselves.

Webster's New World Dictionary defines esteem as "to value highly; respect; to consider; favorable opinion."[1]

Throughout this book we have seen that God's will is for us to fulfill the charge given to us for *all* men and women. When we let go of the *"selfish ambition or conceit"* that Philippians 2:3 speaks of and begin to place others above ourselves, then we are doing things God's way.

Why is that important? When we do things according to God's commands, then we will truly have the blessing of God in all that we do. I see over and over again from the Word of God that the way of Joel Landis is not always the way of the Lord. Friend, if you want to get blessed, bless or give to others (Luke 6:38). If you want to be healed, pray for others (James 5:16). If you want to reap a bountiful harvest in your life, then sow a bountiful harvest in the kingdom (2 Corinthians 9:6). This is a spiritual law that God Himself has set in motion: What you sow into the lives of others, you will reap back in your own life.

A mature life in Christ begins when a person starts to lay down his or her life for the brethren, just as Jesus Himself has done for us. The way to "know" that we have passed from death to life is when we love the brethren (1 John 3:13-16). When we stop doing things our way and do them God's way—*for His sake and the Gospel's*—then we will truly see the "hundredfold" come to pass in the church of Jesus Christ.

Jesus told His followers that everyone who had left anything behind to follow Him would receive in this life a hundredfold and, in the age to come, eternal life (Mark 10:29-30). Peter and the other disciples had left all they had to follow the Son of God. They did not do so for their own sakes, but for the sake of Jesus and the Gospel. What are your motives for leaving behind your old life? Better yet, what is your motive in your giving? Is it only for your own sake? Or is it for the purpose of Jesus and increasing His kingdom in the earth?

Remember the Prisoners

In our self-seeking and self-pleasing, it seems that the church has read right over the Scripture that opened this chapter, which is found in all of our Bibles. Do you recall what it says? *"Remember the prisoners as if chained with them—those who are mistreated—since you yourselves are in the body also."*

Are we remembering the prisoners as if chained with them? Do we remember those who are mistreated? We in the body of Christ—especially in Western society—seem like we sometimes lose touch with reality. We just cruise along in our own little bubbles, not realizing that there is a whole other world out there beyond our own personal interests.

Many Christians throughout the earth have been imprisoned simply because of their faith in Jesus and because of their decision to hold fast to their confession of Christ as Lord. Many believers throughout the nations are being mistreated because of their faith in God.

During the apostle Paul's life, he himself was imprisoned many times for the sake of the Gospel. When writing to the Colossians, he asked them to *"remember my chains"* (Colossians 4:18). Paul experienced firsthand what it was like to be mistreated and locked up in a prison cell. It was not a good place to be. In New Testament times the prisons were dark, cold, damp and very unfriendly dungeons.

No one in his right mind would want to stay for any length of time in any prison that I have ever heard about in this world. Neither did the apostle Paul want to be forgotten and left on his own during his times of imprisonment for preaching the Gospel. Many Christians throughout the world today held captive by prison bars are hoping that we the body of Christ have not forgotten them as they languish in the hands of unreasonable men.

Yet, have we not only forgotten our imprisoned brothers and sisters, but also shut our eyes and ears to their cries for help? Have we once again forgotten to put the charge into action for *all* men, including the prisoners who are part of the body of Christ?

Chapter 13 of Hebrews begins with this statement: *"Let brotherly love continue."* Verse 3 then goes on to say, *"Remember the prisoners as if chained with them—those who are mistreated."* But the verse doesn't end there; it continues, *"since you yourselves are in the body also."*

God wants us to see ourselves standing with our brethren. He wants us to know that when any of the saints are being imprisoned or mistreated because of the Gospel of Jesus Christ, we are right there with them in their time of trial. Think about it. As you are reading the words on this page, you too are chained alongside your imprisoned brethren.

In the natural this doesn't make sense. But I hope it is making biblical sense to you. God wants us to realize that we must be concerned about the well-being of the whole body of Christ.

First Corinthians 12:12-27 says this about the members of the body of Christ:

> *For as the body is one and has many members, but all the members of that one body, being many, are one body, so also is Christ. For by one Spirit we were all baptized into one body—whether Jews or Greeks, whether slaves or free—and have all been made to drink into one Spirit. For in fact the body is not one member but many. If the foot should say, "Because I am not a hand, I am not of the body," is it therefore not of the body? And if the ear should say, "Because I am not an eye, I am not of the body," is it therefore not of the body? If the whole body were an eye, where would be the hearing? If the whole were hearing, where would be the smelling? But*

> *now God has set the members, each one of them, in the body just as He pleased. And if they were all one member, where would the body be? But now indeed there are many members, yet one body. And the eye cannot say to the hand, "I have no need of you"; nor again the head to the feet, "I have no need of you." No, much rather, those members of the body which seem to be weaker are necessary. And those members of the body which we think to be less honorable, on these we bestow greater honor; and our unpresentable parts have greater modesty, but our presentable parts have no need. But God composed the body, having given greater honor to that part which lacks it, that there should be no schism in the body, but that the members should have the same care for one another. And if one member suffers, all the members suffer with it; or if one member is honored, all the members rejoice with it. Now you are the body of Christ, and members individually.*

Once again these are words given to us by Paul. He had gotten a revelation of what Christianity is all about, which is this: There is only one body and in it are many members. The church is called the body of Christ, and like the human body it has many parts—of which each and every one of them is important in its function. Paul also said that the members should have the same care for one another. A dysfunctional body part is one that does not care for the rest of the body. Let's not be dysfunctional Christians. As a part of the body of Christ, it is our job to care about others in the body.

According to this Scripture, if one member suffers, *all* the members suffer with it. In other words, if there is one solitary believer someplace in this world who is suffering, then whether or not you are aware of it, the whole rest of the body is affected along with that person. We all like to rejoice with the member who is honored, but how do we respond to the member of the body who suffers or is imprisoned for "the cause"?

Did you notice, while you were reading this passage from 1 Corinthians 12, that God is the one who sets each and every one of us in the body just as He pleases? You and I are what we are today because of God. And we all have a part to play in God's plan in this earth.

Fighting for Deliverance

Part of our task is to fight the good fight of faith. Satan is doing all he can to stop the bearers of the Good News from preaching the Gospel. If he could get away with it, he would drag off every preacher and believer of the Gospel to a prison cell to be killed just as he did in the days of Saul of Tarsus. But I do not believe Satan will accomplish his goals in this generation. Why? Because I believe this generation will rise up and fulfill the charge "first of all"! Then we will see God's will come to pass, which is "*that all men be saved and come to the knowledge of the truth.*"

Paul exhorted us first of all to make supplications, prayers, intercessions and giving of thanks for all men, for kings and all who are in authority, so that *we* may lead quiet and peaceable lives in all godliness and reverence!

That "we" is the body of Christ with all its members! God's will is for His people to lead quiet and peaceable lives, with *all* godliness and reverence! It is time for the saints of God to go to war, not against flesh and blood, but in the spiritual realm to fight for the lives of those whom Satan is trying to destroy.

Here is a biblical example of how God came through for Paul in his life:

> *For we do not want you to be ignorant, brethren, of our trouble which came to us in Asia: that we were burdened beyond measure, above strength, so that we despaired even of life. Yes, we had the sentence of death in ourselves, that we should not trust in ourselves but in God who raises the dead, who delivered us from so great a death, and does deliver us; in whom we trust that He will still deliver us, you also helping together in prayer for us, that thanks may be given by many persons on our behalf for the gift granted to us through many.* 2 Corinthians 1:8-11

Paul and those involved in the Gospel with him trusted in the God who raised the dead! He had no reason to fear death when serving the God who overcomes death. I don't know about your god, but my God raises the dead! He is an awesome God! He is a *deliverer*!

In verse 10, Paul mentioned three things about God:

- He delivered us from so great a death—*past tense.*

- He does deliver us—*present tense.*
- And we trust that He will deliver us—*future tense.*

In all three tenses Paul said that God delivers us! The only thing we have to do is believe Him. Why? God works with our faith. Jesus said what we have to do is *"believe"* (John 6:29).

Paul also pointed out that the Corinthian church helped them in their deliverance by their prayers. In Acts 12 when Herod imprisoned Peter, the church began to pray and remained in *constant prayer* until God moved and Peter "came home." In the same way, God desires us to pray to bring about all the changes necessary to cause freedom to come in the lives of men. If there are members of the body of Christ in chains, we must pray, intercede and give thanks until the prisoners are released, the jailers and their households are saved and the kingdom of God is increased in the earth. We must not ignore this command or be apathetic. We must join forces with our brothers and sisters and fight with them for their lives and that of others.

Can we be like those Hebrews during the time of Nehemiah the prophet who rebuilt the walls of Jerusalem even while their enemies made plans to attack them? They were watching and praying and working all at the same time. Nehemiah wrote, *"Do not be afraid....Remember the Lord, great and awesome, and fight for your brethren, your sons, your daughters, your wives, and your houses"* (Nehemiah 4:14b).

We have no need to be afraid.

> *Yet in all these things we are more than conquerors through Him who loved us.* Romans 8:37

It would have been great if God had just called us "conquerors" through Him, but He went even further than that and said we are *"more than conquerors"* through Him. That is what God says about you and I who are in Christ!

It is time for believers to declare to the kingdom of darkness that, in Christ, "We are more than conquerors!" We will remember our brothers and sisters in bondage and in prison; we will pray for all men and push back the forces of darkness that are at work in the earth!

Endnote

1. David B. Guralnik, ed, *Webster's New World Dictionary of the American Language* (New York: Warner Books, 1979), p. 210.

Chapter 7

A Generation That Gives Thanks for All Men

First, I thank my God through Jesus Christ for you all....without ceasing I make mention of you always in my prayers. Romans 1:8-9

I thank my God always concerning you.... 1 Corinthians 1:4

We give thanks to the God and Father of our Lord Jesus Christ, praying always for you. Colossians 1:3

We give thanks to God always for you all, making mention of you in our prayers. 1 Thessalonians 1:2

We are bound to thank God always for you, brethren.... 2 Thessalonians 1:3

I thank God, whom I serve with a pure conscience...without ceasing I remember you in my prayers night and day... 2 Timothy 1:3

I thank my God, making mention of you always in my prayers. Philemon 4

In the charge that the apostle Paul gave to the church, he said that in our making of supplications, prayers and intercessions, we also are to be giving thanks to God for all men.

It is evident, from the Scriptures just quoted, that Paul was indeed a man who practiced what he preached!

Often, in the beginning of many of the letters he wrote, he informed the reader(s) that not only was he continually praying for them, but in his praying and making of supplications he also was thanking God for them. When you look closely at his texts, you'll see that he was not just simply thanking God for them; he was thanking God for what He was doing in their lives.

Just in case you need to be reminded, we are not supposed to be complaining to God about other people. Rather, we are to see them as God sees them and in our times of prayer we need to talk about them as Jesus would. Just think about the popular acronym, "WWJD"—"What Would Jesus Do?" What would He say about others in His time of prayer or giving of thanks?

Mixing Joy and Thanks With Prayer

Rejoice in the Lord always. Again I will say, rejoice! Let your gentleness be known to all men. The Lord is at hand. Be anxious for nothing, but in everything by prayer and supplication, with thanksgiving, let your requests be made known to God; and the peace of God, which surpasses all understanding, will guard your hearts and minds through Christ Jesus. Philippians 4:4-7

See that no one renders evil for evil to anyone, but always pursue what is good both for yourselves and for all. Rejoice always, pray without ceasing, in everything give thanks; for this is the will of God in Christ Jesus for you. 1 Thessalonians 5:15-18

I am sure you have heard preached and taught the Scripture that says God loves a *"cheerful giver"* (2 Corinthians 9:7). Did you know that God also enjoys those who mix rejoicing and giving of thanks to Him in their praying? According to these two passages from Philippians and 1 Thessalonians, letters Paul had written to the churches, we are to *"rejoice always"*—and this would include in the time we spend in prayers and supplications as we make our requests known to God.

Philippians 4:4-7 says that when you pray, and mix rejoicing and thanksgiving with it, that *"the peace of God, which surpasses all understanding, will guard your hearts and minds."* The passage of 1 Thessalonians 5:15-18 says that such *"is the will of God in Christ Jesus for you."*

If you don't know what God's will is for your life, please re-read these verses. The will of God in Christ Jesus for *you* is to rejoice always, pray without ceasing (non-stop) and give thanks in everything.

Stop wondering and worrying about God's will! Just do these things—this is God's will for you and I. I believe that if we will obey in these things, then all the other things in God's plan for our lives will unfold. Satan cannot stand happy or rejoicing Christians, thankful Christians or Christians who pray. What do you think Satan would do about you if you are constantly rejoicing, praying and thanking God? He would probably leave you alone! He simply cannot stand hearing joy and thanksgiving coming out of the mouths and hearts of the saints of God. It reflects God! Psalm 22:3 (KJV) says that God inhabits the praises of His people. Do you want to get rid of the devil? Just let God come and inhabit your life. Satan always loses when God's people praise Him regardless of circumstances and situations.

If you still are not convinced of the importance of giving thanks and rejoicing while praying, take a look at one more example that Paul wrote down by the Holy Spirit, found in Philippians 1:1-11:

> *Paul and Timothy, bondservants of Jesus Christ, to all the saints in Christ Jesus who are in Philippi, with the bishops and deacons: Grace to you and peace from God our Father and the Lord Jesus Christ. I thank my God upon every remembrance of you, always in every prayer of mine making request for you all with joy, for your fellowship in the gospel from the first day until now, being confident of this very thing, that He who has begun a good work*

in you will complete it until the day of Jesus Christ; just as it is right for me to think this of you all, because I have you in my heart, inasmuch as both in my chains and in the defense and confirmation of the gospel, you all are partakers with me of grace. For God is my witness, how greatly I long for you all with the affection of Jesus Christ. And this I pray, that your love may abound still more and more in knowledge and all discernment, that you may approve the things that are excellent, that you may be sincere and without offense till the day of Christ, being filled with the fruits of righteousness which are by Jesus Christ, to the glory and praise of God.

Once again we see how Paul wrote to the the saints in Christ Jesus that he was thanking God in every remembrance of them in his prayers and making requests for all of them with joy!

Paul was not just doing this for the leaders (the bishops and deacons at Philippi), but for the whole of the church there. Every time he remembered them in his praying he was thanking God for them, and doing so with joy. In verse 5 he said that he had been doing this from the beginning of their fellowship in the Gospel right up until the day he wrote the letter that has become the New Testament book of Philippians.

Earlier we looked at how God sees things and how He wants us to come into agreement with His Word and by faith to believe that what He has said is the truth.

It is an act of faith to thank God for what He is doing in the lives of others. Paul said that he made such acts of faith for all of those at Philippi.

So often it can be easier for us to complain to God about people or even write them off our prayer lists because of what we think they should do or not do. From what we can tell regarding Paul's words, he spoke only good things about all these people in his time of bringing them to God in prayer. In verse 6 he said he was confident that Jesus would complete the work He had begun in them. He wasn't "hoping" or "wishing" anything for them here; rather, he was *confident* that Jesus would see that His will was carried out in them.

Verses 9-11 of Philippians 1 say that Paul was praying this for them: *"that your love may abound still more and more in knowledge and all discernment, that you may approve the things that are excellent, that you may be sincere and without offense till the day of Christ, being filled with the fruits of righteousness which are by Jesus Christ.*" Paul was going for the gusto in his prayer for them! He was believing for God's best to come to pass in their lives. He even went as far as saying that he was praying they would be *"without offense"* right up until the return of Jesus. This is almost too good to be true, but do you know what? It is true!

Are we as Christians praying this way for other fellow brothers and sisters in the body of Christ today? Are we following the Word of God that says we should "first of all" pray for all men, that we may live lives that are quiet and peaceable, in all reverence and godliness? Many Christians have been *preying* on other Christians instead of praying God's blessings on them according to the Word of God.

I don't know about you, but I want men and women of God to pray for me like Paul did every time they remember me in their prayers.

In verse 7 Paul said that the saints were partakers with him of grace. Church, we are all partakers together of God's grace. It is time that we choose to walk in the love of God and to express His grace to others. It is time for a generation of God's people to stop the bickering and fighting and get on with God. Can we, like Paul, pray good things for others? Can we ask the Father to bring about His very best for them? Could we go way out on a limb and believe that God could help each and every one of those we pray for to be without offense until the coming of the Lord? Can we believe that Jesus can complete all that He has begun to do by His own great power and ability working in the lives of our brothers and sisters in the Lord?

Right Thinking

As soon as Paul had finished the words, *"being confident of this very thing, that He who has begun a good work in you will complete it until the day of Jesus Christ,"* he wrote, *"it is right for me to think this of you all, because I have you in my heart."*

The New American Standard Bible words it like this: *"For it is only right for me to feel this way about you all."* The King James Version uses the Old

English word *meet* in its translating of the Greek word *dikaios.*[1] Dake's Annotated Reference Bible defines *dikaios* as "just or righteous."[2]

Paul was doing the right thing, not the wrong thing, by being confident that Jesus would complete or perform the good work that He began in them.

Why was it right? *"Because I have you in my heart."* Paul had such a Godly love for the churches and for all the saints that he had them in his heart. I believe that God had given him a new heart attitude for the people of God. It is truly amazing to see how God took a man who was persecuting and hating Christians and made him into a man who loved and cared about other Christians probably more than he cared about his own well-being at times. I really don't believe that there is anyone too hard-hearted or too cold-hearted or any other kind of "hearted" for God to do a miracle in his or her life and change that person into a new creation believer whom He can use for His purposes and kingdom.

Just as a caterpillar is transformed into a butterfly and a tadpole into a frog, God can bring about supernatural change in the life of any man or woman, boy or girl.

I believe that, like Paul, you and I have many we hold in our hearts. What are we doing when they come to our remembrance? Are we thanking God upon every remembrance? Or are we giving them over to the devil in what we say with our mouths about them?

What we say is so very important. Proverbs 18:20-21 says, *"A man's stomach shall be satisfied from the fruit of his mouth; from the produce of his lips he shall be filled. Death and life are in the power of the tongue, and those who love it will eat its fruit."*

According to the Word of God, our words produce fruit that bring forth either life or death. Jesus, the Word of God, said this:

> *For out of the abundance of the heart the mouth speaks. A good man out of the good treasure of his heart brings forth good things, and an evil man out of the evil treasure brings forth evil things. But I say to you that for every idle word men may speak, they will give account of it in the day of judgment. For by your words you will be justified, and by your words you will be condemned.* Matthew 12:34b-37

Jesus wants us to be as a good man, with a good treasure in our heart who speaks forth good things. It is very important to God that we speak that which is good. It is so important to Him, in fact, that He said for every idle (which means vain or useless) word we may speak, we will give account of it to Him one day. In case you didn't know it, your words will justify you or condemn you.

Jesus also said, *"He who believes in Me, as the Scripture has said, out of his heart* [the King James Version says 'belly'] *will flow rivers of living water"* (John 7:38). I believe that Jesus was referring to the Scripture in Proverbs 4:20-23 when He said this concerning a believer's heart and the rivers of living water that would come forth out of his or her inner man:

> *My son, give attention to my words; incline your ear to my sayings. Do not let them depart from your eyes; keep them in the midst of your heart; for they are life to those who find them, and health to all their flesh. Keep your heart with all diligence, for out of it spring the issues of life.*

Not only does God give us a new heart when we are born again, but He also places His Holy Spirit in us. Why? God wants to put His Word in our hearts and then He wants to bring it forth as *"rivers of living water."* Out of our hearts should be springing forth the issues of life—God's life.

Are you, as a believer, allowing the Holy Spirit to bring forth rivers of living water out of your heart? Are you thanking God for those you are praying for? Are you convinced, like Paul was, that God can and will perform and complete all that He began to do in their lives? Speak what God would say about them; His will is good, acceptable and perfect (Romans 12:2)!

Do you remember what the angels declared at Jesus' birth? *"On earth peace, goodwill toward men"* (Luke 2:14). God wants to bring peace in people's lives and bring to pass His good will in them. Can He use us in our times of prayer? Are you mixing joy and giving thanks in your praying? Are you thinking the right things about those you have in your heart? By the power of His Holy Spirit, you can—let the river flow!

Endnotes

1. James Strong, *Strong's Exhaustive Concordance of the Bible* (Nashville, Tennessee: Holman Bible Publishers, n.d.), #G1342.
2. Finis Jennings Dake, *Dake's Annotated Reference Bible,* Large Note Edition (Lawrenceville, Georgia: Dake Bible Sales, Inc., 1961, 1963, 1981), p. 215 NT.

PART III

For Kings

Chapter 8

A Generation That Puts the Government Upon His Shoulders

For unto us a Child is born, unto us a Son is given; and the government will be upon His shoulder. And His name will be called Wonderful, Counselor, Mighty God, Everlasting Father, Prince of Peace. Of the increase of His government and peace there will be no end, upon the throne of David and over His kingdom, to order it and establish it with judgment and justice from that time forward, even forever. The zeal of the Lord of hosts will perform this. Isaiah 9:6-7

Isaiah, the prophet of God, prophesied this about the coming Messiah 700 years before Jesus' birth. It is the prophetic foretelling of Jesus' coming to earth. This one who is coming will be both a child that is born and a Son that is given. God Himself will come as a child, born here as a baby. He will be the God/Man who will bring an unending kingdom of peace on this earth.

I am sure that you know the Christmas story, as we call it today, so I'll just summarize.

Approximately 2,000 years ago Gabriel, an angel of God, appeared to a young woman named Mary. He told her, *"The Holy Spirit will come upon you, and the power of the Highest will overshadow you; therefore, also, that Holy One who is to be born will be called the Son of God"* (Luke 1:35).

This same angel (messenger) appeared to Joseph and told him, *"Do not be afraid to take to you Mary your wife, for that which is conceived in her is of the Holy Spirit. And she will bring forth a Son, and you shall call His name JESUS, for He will save His people from their sins"* (Matthew 1:20-21).

The next two verses say, *"So all this was done that it might be fulfilled which was spoken by the Lord through the prophet, saying: 'Behold, the virgin shall be with child, and bear a Son, and they shall call His name Immanuel,' which is translated, 'God with us'* " (Matthew 1:22-23; see also Isaiah 7:14).

Jesus was this Child and this Son. He was Immanuel, "God with us."

Did you notice that when the "Christ" (Jesus) was born here on earth, the Scriptures say that His government and peace would increase and not end? The prophetic Word of God also spoke of another characteristic of His coming, one that we want to look at more closely in this chapter: *"The government will be upon His shoulder."*

Too often this sentence gets kind of lost in all the rest of the proclamation concerning the coming Messiah. We celebrate His name—Wonderful, Counselor, Mighty God, Everlasting Father, Prince of Peace. In fact, one of the greatest musical works of all time, *Handel's Messiah*, rings out those words. Can you hear them even now?

I guess the part that says *"the government shall be upon His shoulder"* isn't quite so exciting to us. "The government shall be upon His shoulder" is a great lyric when you take the time to ponder it.

Before we continue, though, let's establish some facts about the church's place and Jesus' place together.

The Body and the Head

Jesus' birth on the earth was the beginning of the New Covenant coming to fruition. God was in the process of making a way for mankind to become "one" with Him—for Him to be with us and us to be with Him (John 17:20-23).

Through Jesus' death, burial and resurrection, He was creating the church, which the Word of God also calls "the body of Christ" or "the body in Christ" (Romans 12:5; 1 Corinthians 10:16-17; 12:27; Ephesians 1:22-23).

The true church of Jesus Christ includes all who are part of the body of Christ. Those who are not saved, those who have not yet come to the knowledge of the truth, should be able to see Christ Himself being expressed in and through our lives and within our churches. This is God's desire for His church. This is why He gave gifts to the church.

> *He Himself gave some to be apostles, some prophets, some evangelists, and some pastors and teachers, for the equipping* [KJV, perfecting] *of the saints for the work of ministry, for the edifying of the body of Christ, till we all come to the unity of the faith and of the knowledge of the Son of God, to a perfect man, to the measure of the stature of the fullness of Christ.* Ephesians 4:11-13

Brothers and sisters, we are to be looking more and more like Christ being manifested here in the earth! According to this Scripture it takes all the five-fold gifts—apostles, prophets, evangelists, pastors and teachers to bring about all that is included in the fullness in Christ in our lives. Who are the apostles and prophets? Who are the evangelists and pastors? And who are the teachers that God is using in your life?

The Scriptures clearly state that the church is the body, and the head of that body is Jesus.

> *And He is the head of the body, the church, who is the beginning, the firstborn from the dead, that in all things He may have the preeminence.* Colossians 1:18

> *And He put all things under His feet, and gave Him to be head over all things to the church, who is His body, the fullness of Him who fills all in all.* Ephesians 1:22-23

Christ is head of the church; and He is the Savior of the body. Ephesians 5:23b

The body of Christ has only one Head—Jesus. That means everything below the Head is the body, which is the church! From the neck on down, as far as the symbolism used in the Word of God goes, you and I and all believers are the body of Christ.

Upon His Shoulder

Knowing who the body is and who the Head is, is significant when you look at this phrase of Isaiah 9:6: *"the government will be upon His shoulder."* The word used for "shoulder" here is the Hebrew word *shekem*, which means "the neck (between the shoulders) as the place of burdens," according to *Strong's Exhaustive Concordance.*[1]

When you look at Isaiah 9:6 in its fulfillment in Christ's coming, in the light of the New Testament or New Covenant, could this verse be saying that the "government" of this world will be under His Head or authority and resting upon His shoulder, which is the body of Christ, the church in the earth?

If this is true, then all the government that exists in the earth is subject to Jesus Christ.

This is what God says about it in Colossians 1:16-17:

For by Him all things were created that are in heaven and that are on earth, visible and invisible, whether thrones or dominions or principalities or powers. All things were created through Him and for Him. And He is before all things, and in Him all things consist.

According to this Scripture, all government—seen and even unseen in the spirit realm—is under His authority. Look at Colossians 2:9-10:

For in Him dwells all the fullness of the Godhead bodily; and you are complete in Him, who is the head of all principality and power.

There is that word *all* again—once more speaking of *all* principality and power in the universe. It is all under Jesus! There is not one thing happening in the universe that God is unaware of. There is not one king, president or emperor who sits upon any throne or in any place of authority whom Jesus Himself has not allowed to be in that position. There is no one in any position of authority on this earth whom Jesus does not know about. In fact, this Scripture tells us that not only does He know about them, but He Himself also created them.

Have you ever taken the time to see people through the eyes of God? Every man, woman, boy and girl was created by Jesus! Jesus' will is that all of His creation would come to know Him, serve Him and be part of His kingdom. Even those whom we view as enemies of God, He loves and cares about. Second Peter 3:9 says that the Lord is not willing that any should perish.

In Chapter 10 we will check out how God views kings, rulers and the other earthly authorities. (I'll give you a hint: He looks at them in a way that is very different from the way we tend to see them.) God is a God of faith, and we are called to be people of faith. God's desire is that we would see others through His perspective. But for now I want you to see that not only is the government under the headship of Christ, but it also is "*upon His shoulder.*" In other words, it rests upon us—the body, the church. That means we support it, that we are to carry it. We are to pray for it. And as we submit ourselves to the authorities above us, those authorities will submit themselves to the Lordship of Jesus.

In the past many have fought against the authority above them. That is what the first rebel, Satan, did. Rather than submit to God as the "Highest" or "Immanent One," he rebelled and became the enemy of God. Satan is a rebellious spirit; he is always trying to cause God's creation to rebel against the authority of God or His Word. Satan also is trying to cause mankind to rebel against any and all forms of authority. For innumerable ages he has succeeded in causing men to rebel against those who have God-given authority. He causes children to rebel against the parents' authority in the home. He constantly attempts to get the body of Christ to fight against other people. (We discussed this in an earlier chapter.) He wants us to attack men, God's creation like ourselves, but it is time for a generation of Christians to recognize who the enemy is and to drive him out! We must drive him out of the atmosphere that surrounds us.

It is time for a generation of Christians to pray for the people they see and to bring about change in the leaders who sit in positions of authority. Scripture says that the support of government rests upon the shoulder of the body of Christ! At the same time, we must keep in mind that the true fight is in the realm of the unseen. Ephesians 2:2 mentions *"the prince of the power of the air, the spirit that now worketh in the children of disobedience"* (KJV). Let's take a moment here and look more closely at that passage in context and notice where we all "once walked":

> *And you He made alive, who were dead in trespasses and sins, in which you once walked according to the course of this world, according to the prince of the power of the air, the spirit who now works in the sons of disobedience, among whom also we all once conducted ourselves in the lusts of our flesh, fulfilling the desires of the flesh and of the mind, and were by nature children of wrath, just as the others. But God, who is rich in mercy, because of His great love with which He loved us, even when we were dead in trespasses, made us alive together with Christ (by grace you have been saved).* Ephesians 2:1-5

We all were in the same situation; we all were under the control of Satan at one time. But now we have been redeemed! And with that redemption, God has given us authority as the body of Christ under Jesus, our Head, the Lord of lords and King of kings! It is time for Christians to pray for the governments of this world. It is time to exercise the authority over the powers of the air that God has given us and pray!

I'm sure you have heard the phrase, "prayer changes things." That is absolutely the truth. The prayer of the saints of God, the prayer of God's children, the prayers of you and I can move mountains. Why? Because we are God's children (1 John 3:2)! And as God's children, like "God and Company," we work together with God in our time of prayer. We are not hoping for some distant cosmic force to respond to our prayers. We are bringing our requests, our petitions, our intercessions to our heavenly Father who loves us as well as this world. It is more than a cliché.

> *For God so loved the world, that he gave his only begotten Son, that whosoever believeth in him should not perish, but have everlasting life.*
> John 3:16 KJV

Will you be part of the generation that rises up in the authority of the body of Christ to pray for and support government?

Endnote

1. James Strong, *Strong's Exhaustive Concordance of the Bible* (Nashville, Tennessee: Holman Bible Publishers, n.d.), #H7926.

Chapter 9

A Generation That Honors the King

HONOR: High regard or respect; adherence to principles considered right; integrity; something done or given as a token of respect.[1]

First Peter 2 is full of many verses that we quote to bring encouragement, hope and strength to our faith. Most of the statements made in this chapter are written in long sentences—except for those in verse 17. It is almost as if another writer took over Peter's pen for a moment. This is what it says in this verse:

> *Honor all people. Love the brotherhood. Fear God. Honor the king.*
> 1 Peter 2:17

One verse, eleven words, four profound statements.

If Christians and those who are "not yet" Christians could do just these four things, we would be doing good. I mean, really good.

We today live in a world that has moved far from these biblical ideals. Giving honor is becoming a lost art in America.

As terrible as 9-11 was, some good has come about since that terrorist act happened in 2001. If nothing else, today Americans are more apt to give honor and respect to those to whom it is due, especially to firefighters, police officers and other rescue workers who became "heroes" in the aftermath of the collapse of the World Trade Towers in New York City. In addition, our nation is once again giving respect and honor to our Armed Forces in their fight against terrorism.

So when the Word of God tells us to honor all people, then that is what we should do. I believe that includes even the small ways of showing respect or honor. For instance, we need to restore the use of words like "Yes, sir," or "No, sir," and "Yes, ma'am," or "No, ma'am," etc. Courtesy in small areas goes a long way. In fact, Peter also told us as Christians to be courteous (1 Peter 3:8). Respect, honor, courtesy—these are to be part of our Christian lifestyle. You see, Christianity is not just a bunch of religious activities; it is a way of living that does the practical things as well as the spiritual things. Look again at what Peter said we are to do.

First, we are to honor all people.

Second, we are to love the brotherhood. We love other Christians despite our differences.

Third, we are to fear God.

Fourth, we are to honor the king.

Honor the King

We may be able to justify doing the first three, but honor the king? Sometimes we have a hard time with that one. Nevertheless, Peter gave no options here. These are commands. And I believe that if you disobey God's commands, you can cut off the blessings of the Lord in your life or even in the body of Christ.

You may ask, "But what if he is really a rotten leader?" The answer from God is, "Honor the king." In America we have a president and a vice-president. We have senators and congressmen who together make up our nation's government. They are our "king" in this land in this age. We do not have a dictator or single ruler who makes all of the decisions. We have a plurality. And that means we honor all who walk in those roles.

It is a sad thing that many of us do not even know who the people in authority are whom we are to honor and pray for. Remember the charge "first of all"? Do you know who your senators and congressmen are? Do you know who your state legislators are? Do you know who your local officials are? Who is the mayor of your town? Christians, we need to know who these people are, and we need to pray for them!

Of course, honoring a leader does not mean idolizing him or her. The Word of God does not say to worship the king. There is quite a difference between honor and worship. Several kings throughout the Bible wanted the people in their kingdoms not only to respect them or honor them, but also to worship them as a god. However, we do not have an obligation to worship any man or ruler, other than the Lord God Himself. We *do* have an obligation to honor them and pray for them. And one way we can honor our leaders is by how we speak of them.

Honor With Our Mouths

A lot of things were spoken in the last decade or so that have been dishonoring to our king (president), especially during the presidency of Bill Clinton. Many Christians jumped on the bandwagon against him and spoke a lot of verbal abuse. Maybe he was doing some things you didn't agree with, but were you continually praying for him? Were you making supplication to God for him? Were you interceding for him and giving thanks to God for him during his eight years of office as president?

Were you honoring him or dishonoring him? If you have a complaint about anyone, you need to take that person to the Highest Authority—Jesus.

The apostle James had this to say about our tongues and the words that come out of our mouths:

> *With it we bless our God and Father, and with it we curse men, who have been made in the similitude of God. Out of the same mouth proceed blessing and cursing. My brethren, these things ought not to be so. Does a spring send*

forth fresh water and bitter from the same opening? Can a fig tree, my brethren, bear olives, or a grapevine bear figs? Thus no spring yields both salt water and fresh. James 3:9-12

We are to be blessing others with the words that come out of our mouths. Do we really want to live quiet and peaceable lives? Let's respond to what we see and hear according to the Word of the Lord. If you are not happy with your king, tell God about it. Take it to the Lord. Ask Him to bring about the changes necessary. After all, it is God's will that the king *"be saved and...come to the knowledge of the truth"*—isn't that what 1 Timothy 2:4 says?

At the time of this writing, George W. Bush is the President of the United States of America. Whether or not you agree with his policies and actions, he is the president, and God requires that we honor him. Speaking of honor, our president is not just "George W." He has a title, "President George W. Bush," and if we continuously refuse to use his title when referring to him, it could be an indication of a disrespectful heart attitude. God says we cannot hold on to that. Before we go on, I want to remind you that we do not fight or wrestle against flesh and blood. That means our leaders are not the problem. There are spiritual forces that use men at times to bring about Satan's plans or will in the earth. We must recognize this and pray for the man or woman in a position of authority and do all that is in our power, putting on the whole armor of God and standing against the attack of the enemy in that leader's life.

Are you honoring the king? Have you blessed him today? According to the Scriptures, this is how we honor the king:

- We make prayers for him.
- We make supplications to God for him.
- We make intercession (praying in the Spirit) for him.
- We give thanks to God for him.

If we think he is in error, then we ask God to change him. If we think he is in sin, we ask God to reveal it to him and bring about Godly repentance. If we think he is doing *everything* wrong, then we ask God to bring good and Godly counsel to him. And no matter what, we thank God for him; we thank

God for bringing about change in his life. Use your faith in this! Begin to see your leader as God sees him.

How would God see him? Read on and you'll find out...

You shall not revile God, nor curse a ruler of your people. Exodus 22:28

...For it is written, "You shall not speak evil of a ruler of your people." Acts 23:5

Christian, will you rise up to fulfill the charge? Will you be part of the generation that prays for and honors all people, including leaders and those in authority?

Endnote

1. David B. Guralnik, ed., *Webster's New World Dictionary of the American Language* (New York: Warner Books, 1979), p. 290.

Chapter 10

A Generation That Sees World Leaders Like God Sees Them: As His Ministers

Let every soul be subject to the governing authorities. For there is no authority except from God, and the authorities that exist are appointed by God. Therefore whoever resists the authority resists the ordinance of God, and those who resist will bring judgment on themselves. For rulers are not a terror to good works, but to evil. Do you want to be unafraid of the authority? Do what is good, and you will have praise from the same. For he is God's minister to you for good. But if you do evil, be afraid; for he does not bear the sword in vain; for he is God's minister, an avenger to execute wrath on him who practices evil. Therefore you must be subject, not only because of wrath but also for conscience' sake. Romans 13:1-5

Remind them to be subject to rulers and authorities, to obey, to be ready for every good work, to speak evil of no one, to be peaceable, gentle, showing all humility to all men. For we ourselves were also once foolish, disobedient, deceived, serving various lusts and pleasures, living in malice and envy, hateful and hating one another. But when the kindness and the love of God our Savior toward man appeared, not by works of righteousness which we have done, but according to His mercy He saved us, through the washing of regeneration and renewing of the Holy Spirit, whom He poured out on us abundantly through Jesus Christ our Savior, that having been justified by His grace we should become heirs according to the hope of eternal life. Titus 3:1-7

Therefore submit yourselves to every ordinance of man for the Lord's sake, whether to the king as supreme, or to governors, as to those who are sent by him for the punishment of evildoers and for the praise of those who do good. For this is the will of God, that by doing good you may put to silence the ignorance of foolish men—as free, yet not using liberty as a cloak for vice, but as bondservants of God. 1 Peter 2:13-16

No, these are not parts of the Constitution of the United States or even our Declaration of Independence. These passages all are found right in the New Testament Scriptures. In these texts we are told to be subject to governing authorities (Romans 13:1), to be subject to rulers and authorities (Titus 3:1) and to submit ourselves to every ordinance of man for the Lord's sake, whether to the king or to governors (1 Peter 2:13-14).

God's people are supposed to willingly obey those in positions of authority, submitting to them and obeying the ordinances that are given by them. We often think the will of God for our lives is unclear, but many times the Scriptures tell us straight out what the will of God is. This is one of those times. First Peter 2:15 says, *"For this is the will of God, that by doing good you may put to silence the ignorance of foolish men."*

No matter what nation you live in, it is always God's will for you to do good. Just do a word search in the Bible for "good," and you will find that we are to do good, be good, and speak good, and that by doing so we affect others with our lives.

Let's do good; let's submit to our governmental leaders with pure hearts, for they are set into place by God Himself.

The Authorities That Exist Are Appointed By God

> *Let every soul be subject to the governing authorities. For there is no authority except from God, and the authorities that exist are appointed by God.* Romans 13:1

This verse, which is the one that opened this chapter, tells us that God appointed and set into place the authorities in the world. For many years I tried my best to ignore this verse and pretty much the whole of the first part of Romans 13. When I would read verse 2, which says, *"whoever resists the authority resists the ordinance of God,"* I would wonder how that could be. How could men like Hitler, Stalin, Castro or even Pilate (the one who sentenced Jesus to die on the cross) be men in such positions of authority and yet be put in that position by God Himself?

Verse 4 actually goes on to say that these rulers are God's ministers. In fact, chapter 13 says it *three times*!

I tried to comprehend this, but it just wasn't working. I knew this had to be a misprint or something. Maybe I could find a Bible out there somewhere that did not include these verses because they were not used in most Greek manuscripts or something. If there is an Authorized Version, I reasoned, perhaps there should be an "Un-Authorized" Version available somewhere.

I didn't find a way out of this dilemma, so instead I tried to ignore the whole first part of chapter 13. And I noticed, over the years, that I wasn't the only one not quoting from Romans 13:1-5 during preaching or teaching from the Word of God.

It seemed wrong to me that God's Word would call men like Hitler, Stalin, Castro and other dictators God's ministers. This seemed so contradictory to God's character and His Word—until one day it all came clear to me. Thanks to the Holy Spirit, I finally began to look at this issue in the light of God's perspective. It all made sense to me when I realized that God sees through eyes of *faith*.

We need to see things in the same way that God Himself sees them. We have to get out of the realm of the senses and get over into the place of faith. Only when we do and see things God's way will we be able to do His will.

Here's what the Holy Spirit showed me.

Chapter 4 Comes Before Chapter 13

When the apostle Paul first wrote the book of Romans, it did not have chapters with numbers and numbered verses. It was simply one letter written to the church at Rome. When the saints in Rome read the letter, they wouldn't have started reading it at chapter 13; they would have started at the beginning. They would have started reading at what we know as chapter 1 and then continued right through until finally coming to this part near the end of the letter.

I think you are probably getting the picture here. When reading this letter, or book, as a whole, before you get to chapter 13 you must first read chapter 4. And Romans chapters 3, 4 and 5 contain many references to faith and how faith works in our lives. Chapter 4 specifically says a lot about Abraham and how God calls him the *"father of us all"* (verse 16) and how we are to walk in the steps of the faith our father Abraham walked in (verse 12).

Let's take a closer look at Abraham's walk of faith and study out the steps we need to take in order to view our leaders with faith, the way God does.

The first part of Romans 4:17-22 quotes from Genesis 17:5, where the story of Abraham is found in the Old Testament. It says:

> *(As it is written, "I have made you a father of many nations") in the presence of Him whom he believed—God, who gives life to the dead and calls those things which do not exist as though they did; who, contrary to hope, in hope believed, so that he became the father of many nations, according*

to what was spoken, "So shall your descendants be." And not being weak in faith, he did not consider his own body, already dead (since he was about a hundred years old), and the deadness of Sarah's womb. He did not waver at the promise of God through unbelief, but was strengthened in faith, giving glory to God, and being fully convinced that what He had promised He was also able to perform. And therefore "it was accounted to him for righteousness."

How did Abraham earn such a title as the "Father of us All"?

First, Abraham simply believed that what God had told him was true. He believed, even though it took 25 years from the time God physically came and told him he would have an heir from his own body and his descendants would be innumerable (Genesis 15:3-6) to when Isaac was born.

In Romans Paul talked about how contrary to hope, Abraham in hope believed. He did not consider his own body even though it was *"already dead."* He did not waver at the promise of God through unbelief—but was strengthened in faith, giving glory to God, being fully convinced that what God promised He was also able to perform. He believed God, the God who gives life to the dead and calls those things that do not exist as though they did!

Abraham's Steps of Faith

Let's list out the things Abraham did when he was believing in God, as written in Romans 4:17-22:

- Contrary to hope, in hope he believed.
- Not being weak in faith, he did not consider his own body, already dead.
- He did not waver at the promise of God through unbelief.
- He was strengthened in faith, giving glory to God.
- He was fully convinced that what God promised He was also able to perform.
- He believed in God who gives life to the dead and calls those things that do not exist as though they did.

We can see, then, how having faith in God worked for Abraham and how faith in God should be working presently in all of us who are Abraham's descendants. When it looks hopeless in the realm of the senses, in hope we must believe God. We must choose to not be weak in faith, but like Abraham to not consider our own bodies. (If we let the stuff we live with 24/7 dictate to us, it will weaken our faith.) Like Abraham we must get beyond the circumstances and believe that the promise of God is the truth despite how impossible its fulfillment seems in our own ability.

We cannot waver, or be up and down, with the promises of God through unbelief (see James 1:6-8). Unbelief is one of Satan's biggest tools in keeping us from receiving from the Lord. Unbelief is what kept the children of Israel out of the Promised Land—a *"land flowing with milk and honey"* (Exodus 3:8). Even though the Lord told them to go in and take the land, because of unbelief they did not go in until many years later. As a result, a generation of people did not get to enter the Promised Land.

We need to be strengthened in faith, giving glory to God! Before Abraham held a little baby boy named Isaac in his arms, he was giving glory to God. How do you strengthen your faith while waiting on the promise to be fully manifested in your life? Continue to glorify the Lord. Give thanks to Him for the promises coming to pass even before you are holding them in your arms, whatever they might be.

Be *fully* convinced that what God promised to us, He also is able to perform. This is where "the rubber meets the road" in having faith in God—we must be fully convinced! The Lord asked Sarah this question: *"Is anything too hard for the LORD?"* (Genesis 18:14) This is the million-dollar question, and there is only one answer: absolutely nothing!

The God Whom Abraham Believed

Abraham believed in His God—the one who gives life to the dead, the one who calls those things that do not exist as though they did.

Our God calls those things that do not exist as though they did! He called Abram "*Abraham*" (which means "father of a multitude") even before he was a father. Before there was any physical evidence of Abraham being a daddy, the Lord said to him, "I have made you a father of many nations." Think about it. Not only did Abraham not have any children, but it also would be many years before Abraham's descendants would be a "multitude." First Isaac would have to be born. Then he would have to grow up, have children, and they have children before Abraham could even be considered the "father of a multitude." Meanwhile the years were passing by—and without any evidence, God called Abraham "father of a multitude" and Abraham called himself "father of a multitude." And they were not lying about it; that was the way faith sees things! That is how the God-kind of faith works. God knows the beginning and end of your life and all that happens in between. God knew before Abraham was ever born that when it was all said and done, Abraham would be the father of multitudes.

God gave Abraham a new name to get him over into a realm of faith that would cause him to start seeing himself the way that God saw him.

Faith agrees with the Word of God. Faith calls those things that do not exist as though they did. Faith sees as God sees.[1] Faith does not call things that are as though they do not exist. There is an important distinction here, and I'd like to call your attention to my note at the end of this book where I explain this difference. For now, I just want you to see that we must come into agreement with what God says about those in positions of governmental authority.

God Views World Leaders Through Eyes of Faith

Take stock of what you are saying about world leaders. God does not appreciate ugly talk about them! It is time we begin to see them as God does and talk about them the way He does. According to Jesus, the God-kind of faith has what it says: *"Have faith in God. For assuredly, I say to you, whoever says to this mountain, 'Be removed and be cast into the sea,' and does not doubt in his heart, but believes that those things he says will be done, he will have whatever he says"* (Mark 11:22-23).

This is what God says about world leaders:

"For rulers are not a terror to good works, but to evil." Romans 13:3

"For he is God's minister to you for good. But if you do evil, be afraid; for he does not bear the sword in vain." Romans 13:4a

"For he is God's minister, an avenger to execute wrath on him who practices evil." Romans 13:4b

"They are God's ministers attending continually to this very thing." Romans 13:6

"[They] *are sent by him for the punishment of evildoers and for the praise of those who do good."* 1 Peter 2:14

God, speaking of all authority that exists, said He appoints them and they are His ministers. According to the Highest Authority (God), the rulers praise those who do good and are a "terror" to evil. And if you do evil, be afraid, because they do not bear the sword in vain! A ruler is an avenger to execute wrath on the one who practices evil.

To summarize, God's will is for presidents, kings or emperors—all who are in positions of authority—to be His ministers, approve of that which is good, and punish those who do evil, not bearing the sword in vain.

It would appear that God does in fact believe in capital punishment.

Faith Pays Taxes

If that isn't enough, God also addresses the matter of paying taxes. Romans 13:6-7 says,

For because of this you also pay taxes, for they are God's ministers attending continually to this very thing. Render therefore to all their due: taxes to whom taxes are due, customs to whom customs, fear to whom fear, honor to whom honor.

Did you get happy about paying your taxes lately?

These verses say that when you and I pay taxes, we are giving that money to God's ministers and it is helping them in their fight against evil. The Bible also says that *"God loves a cheerful giver"* (2 Corinthians 9:7)! So if we can agree with the Word of God that our government leaders are "God's ministers," then when we pay taxes we can be cheerful givers, knowing that God can use that money to bless our government and assist them in their job as God's appointed men or women.

I believe that God desires us to give to the federal, state and local authorities that which is due to them. And as we do this with the right heart attitude of obedience to the Lord, He then will make a way for what we give to be given back again to us *"good measure, pressed down, shaken together, and running over"* (Luke 6:38). When Jesus told us to *"give, and it will be given to you,"* He wasn't just telling us to give to Christian organizations. He was telling us to be those who bless others despite all that they might do to us.

Presently many things are going on in government and in the lives of leaders themselves that are contrary to God's ideals. Even though there are such things going on, I believe that God's will is for the church to fulfill the charge given to us *first of all*: to pray, make supplications, make intercessions and give thanks for all men and for all in authority. Our obedience in this matter then enables God to bring about all the changes necessary to cause men and women in government to indeed be His ministers, completing all that He desires to do through them.

God desires that all our leaders on every level, from president to senators to state legislators to governors to supreme court justices to city mayors to city council members, to be saved and come to the knowledge of the truth.

It is time for the saints of God to go to war against the demonic forces, the principalities and powers, the rulers of the darkness of this age, against spiritual hosts of wickedness in the heavenly places. These are the troublemakers who have been using men and women for thousands of years. It is time that we recognize the true forces at work in the lives of men in our cities, our states and our federal and world governments.

Look closely at Ephesians 6:12. It says we are to be warring against *"spiritual hosts of wickedness in the **heavenly places.**"* I believe this is telling us that these wicked beings are in places where they do not belong. It is time for the saints in the army of God to drive them out of any and all the heavenly places!

It is time for the saints of God to go to war on their knees and pray for the flesh and blood leaders in this land. The Christian contemporary band Petra has a song that says, "Get on your knees and fight like a man."[2] Stormie Omartian says in her book, *The Power of Praying Together*, "Praying for our nation is our heritage and it is also our privilege and duty. It's not just for pastors and leaders to do in churches and conferences. It's for you and me to do in some way every day. That's because praying for our nation is not an option. It's a mandate from God."[3] With God in us, with us and for us, we can together bring about supernatural and natural change in this world.

Let me add one more witness from God's holy Word to once again confirm God's will toward this world's leaders:

> *And from Jesus Christ, the faithful witness, the firstborn from the dead, and the ruler over the kings of the earth. To Him who loved us and washed us from our sins in His own blood.* Revelation 1:5

Can you agree with the Word of God? Can you confess what God has already said? Yes indeed, Jesus Christ is the ruler over the kings of the earth! The Word of God does not say that Satan is the ruler over the kings of the earth. *Jesus* is the King of kings and Lord of lords (Revelation 19:16)!

Let's rise up, saints, and be the generation that fulfills the charge regarding our leaders!

Endnotes

1. See Genesis 16:13, *"El-Roi"*
2. Petra, "Get on Your Knees and Fight Like a Man." *This Means War!* Star Song, 1987.
3. Stormie Omartian with Jack Hayford, *The Power of Praying Together* (Eugene, Oregon: Harvest House Publishers, 2003), p. 159.

Chapter 11

A Generation That Sees Unchangeable Decrees Change

It pleased Darius to set over the kingdom an hundred and twenty princes, which should be over the whole kingdom; and over these three presidents; of whom Daniel was first: that the princes might give accounts unto them, and the king should have no damage. Then this Daniel was preferred above the presidents and princes, because an excellent spirit was in him; and the king thought to set him over the whole realm. Then the presidents and princes sought to find occasion against Daniel concerning the kingdom; but they could find none occasion nor fault; forasmuch as he was faithful, neither was there any error or fault found in him. Then said these men, We shall not find any occasion against this Daniel, except we find it against him concerning the law of his God. Then these presidents and princes assembled together to the king, and said thus unto him, King Darius, live for ever. All the presidents of the kingdom, the governors, and the princes, the counsellors, and the captains, have consulted together to establish a royal statute, and to make a firm decree, that whosoever shall ask a petition of any God or man for thirty days, save of thee, O king, he shall be cast into the den of lions. Now, O king, establish the decree, and sign the writing, that it be not changed, according to the law of the Medes and Persians, which altereth not. Wherefore king Darius signed the writing and the decree. Daniel 6:1-9 KJV

This is the preface to the story of Daniel in the lions' den. Not only is this story great Sunday school material, but it also is a wonderful example of how God responds to the prayers and actions of a man who will not compromise his belief in his God even when evil, using men, has conspired against him.

In verses 3 and 4, the princes and the other presidents devised a plan to prevent Daniel from being promoted to a position that would set him over the whole of King Darius' realm. According to the Scriptures, Daniel had an *"excellent spirit"* in him! These conspirators could find nothing wrong with Daniel; he was *faithful* and there was no error or fault found in him. Oh, that the same could be said of us by those who associate with us in this generation!

It is a shame that these governmental leaders in their jealousy pursued such a scheme. Keep in mind that the real villains behind the scenes were satanic forces of darkness. Not only were these forces working to destroy Daniel, but they also were attempting to ruin the king who was being blessed by having such a faithful and God-fearing person working under his leadership.

Concerning the Law of His God

These men (Satan's puppets on a string) came up with a strategy to attack *"the law of his* [Daniel's] *God."* Satan has no new tricks; this is exactly what he is doing in our present age. Satan attacks the "faithful" concerning the law of our God.

When these schemers approached King Darius, they flat-out lied to him. They said, *"**All** the presidents of the kingdom...have consulted together to establish* *a royal statute, and to make a firm decree, that whosoever shall ask a petition of any God or man for thirty days, save of thee, O king, he shall be cast into the den of lions"* (Daniel 6:7 KJV).

Obviously Daniel, one of the three presidents, was not one of the consultants involved in their plan. They lied, and the devil is the father of lies (John 8:44).

The king agreed and went ahead and established the decree. He signed on the dotted line and put into force the law that not only prohibited prayer to God, but also set himself up as a god.

Whenever you try to crush the law of God with a law of man, I can guarantee you that the one true God is concerned about the outcome of such an event.

Verse 8 says that this decree, once made, could not be changed and would not be altered. So, according to man at that time, and according to Satan and his demons at that time, the decree was in force and would not go away. When you look at the same scenario in this present age, currently there are decrees or laws in some nations that are against the people of God, like Daniel, and against the law of our God. Once more, according to men and according to Satan's will, these laws will not be changed.

That is the first part of the story, but thank God that is not the end of the story! Let's read on:

> *Now when Daniel knew that the writing was signed, he went into his house; and his windows being open in his chamber toward Jerusalem, he kneeled upon his knees three times a day, and prayed, and gave thanks before his God, as he did aforetime. Then these men assembled, and found Daniel praying and making supplication before his God. Then they came near, and spake before the king concerning the king's decree; Hast thou not signed a decree, that every man that shall ask a petition of any God or man within thirty days, save of thee, O king, shall be cast into the den of lions? The king answered and said, The thing is true, according to the law of the Medes and Persians, which altereth not. Then answered they and said before the king, That Daniel, which is of the children of the captivity of Judah, regardeth not thee O king, nor the decree that thou hast*

> *signed, but maketh his petition three times a day. Then the king, when he heard these words, was sore displeased with himself, and set his heart on Daniel to deliver him: and he laboured till the going down of the sun to deliver him. Then these men assembled unto the king, and said unto the king, Know, O king, that the law of the Medes and Persians is, That no decree nor statute which the king establisheth may be changed. Then the king commanded, and they brought Daniel, and cast him into the den of lions. Now the king spake and said unto Daniel, Thy God whom thou servest continually, he will deliver thee. And a stone was brought, and laid upon the mouth of the den; and the king sealed it with his own signet, and with the signet of his lords; that the purpose might not be changed concerning Daniel.* Daniel 6:10-17 KJV

I am so glad that Daniel was not your average saint. He was one who knew how to fight back the proper way. He went to war on his knees. He simply did what he already was doing. This was not some kind of panic situation for the man of God; he just *continued doing* what he knew to do.

Daniel did not shrink back. Daniel did not go into hiding. He knew his God. He believed that his God was hearing him when he prayed.

Daniel did not "throw in the towel" and stop praying when he knew the decree had been signed. No, instead of closing the doors and windows and quietly whispering his prayers, he went home and in his upper room with his windows *open* toward Jerusalem, he knelt down on his knees three times that day and prayed and gave thanks before his God, *"as was his custom since early days"* (Daniel 6:10).

The same men who had manipulated the king into putting this new law into action went after Daniel and found him praying and making supplication before his God.

Remember the Charge?

Did you notice that Daniel was praying, making supplications and even giving thanks to his God? He was doing what Paul described centuries later as the charge "first of all."

If you want to live out a life that is quiet and peaceable in all godliness and reverence, respond to pressure like Daniel did. Daniel did not get depressed or down in the dumps. He had a choice to make, and he did the right thing. The devil did not bring him down. Did you notice that when these men found him, he was obviously praying and making supplications to his God? Christians, we do not have to be intimidated by men or demons. We need to be bold in our times of prayer! We also need to be giving thanks in our prayers before God. It might very well have been that Daniel was giving thanks to God for the king or possibly even for the other presidents and princes who were on their way to accuse him in the conspiracy they set in motion.

In verse 15, when accusing Daniel before the king, these men reminded King Darius that the law of the Medes and Persians stated that no decree or statute the king established could be changed. Faced with that, the king gave the command to bring Daniel and put him into the den of lions.

The king was left with no other choice but to see to it that Daniel, the former assistant in government work whom he was just about to promote, was put into the lions' den. (Keep in mind that Daniel was not a practicing lion tamer and these were the man-eating type of cats!) As they were putting Daniel into the den, King Darius told him, *"Your God, whom you serve continually, He will deliver you"* (Daniel 6:16).

King Darius had some of the same patterns in his communication that a lot of our politicians have today. When he was with one crowd he said one thing, and when he was with another he said something else. It looks to me like he was a crowd-pleaser. Unfortunately, a lot of us are like King Darius. Instead, we should be men and women of integrity; we should be people who in conversation our "yes" is "yes" and our "no" is "no" (James 5:12). We should be a people of our word.

Not only had the king signed a decree that could not be changed, but he also put his seal on the stone that covered the way into and out of the lion's den, called *"the mouth of the den"* (Daniel 6:17). The Bible specifically says that the king sealed it, speaking of a document on the stone at the mouth of the den, or possibly on the stone itself, with his signet ring and also with the signet of his lords, *"that the purpose concerning Daniel might not be changed."*

You could say it was "written in stone"—but that is not the end of the story!

> *Then the king went to his palace, and passed the night fasting: neither were instruments of music brought before him: and his sleep went from him. Then the king arose very early in the morning, and went in haste unto the den of lions. And when he came to the den, he cried with a lamentable voice unto Daniel: and the king spake and said to Daniel, O Daniel, servant of the living God, is thy God, whom thou servest continually, able to deliver thee from the lions? Then said Daniel unto the king, "O king, live for ever. My God hath sent his angel, and hath shut the lions' mouths, that they have not hurt me: forasmuch as before him innocency was found in me; and also before thee, O king, have I done no hurt. Then was the king exceeding glad for him, and commanded that they should take Daniel up out of the den. So Daniel was taken up out of the den, and no manner of hurt was found upon him, because he believed in his God. And the king commanded, and they brought those men which had accused Daniel, and they cast them into the den of lions, them, their children, and their wives; and the lions had the mastery of them, and brake all their bones in pieces or ever they came at the bottom of the den.* Daniel 6:18-24 KJV

After a restless night the king went very early in the morning to the den of lions to see if just maybe Daniel's God had come through and preserved him from death. The king cried out to Daniel, *"Daniel, servant of the living God, has your God, whom you serve continually, been able to deliver you from the lions?"* (Daniel 6:20)

What a statement that was. Was this the same man who just put into force a law that placed himself above God? Had he fallen off of his throne on his head or what? Just the day before he was fighting against the God of Daniel, yet the next day he was speaking of Daniel's God as "the living God."

What the king said here contains a very important question. This is the thing that he asked:

> *"Has your God, whom you serve continually, been able to deliver you from the lions?"*

I would like to ask you that same question. *"Has your God, whom you serve continually, been able to deliver you from the lions?"*

Ponder,

ponder,

ponder...

Daniel's God did come through! From within the den of lions came the answer: Daniel replied, *"O king, live forever."*

What an event! Not only was Daniel still alive and well, but his response is noteworthy. He did not say anything threatening or hateful toward the king. Daniel could have replied by saying something like, "Yes, my God did deliver me from these lions, but He is not going to deliver you when I get my hands on you! Prepare to die!"

Why did he answer like he did? I have found in my own experience that if you are praying for someone on a regular basis and you get into that place of faith where you are giving thanks to God for and about someone, it becomes hard to respond to that person in a negative way. Our love of God toward that person only grows stronger as we pray concerning him or her. I believe that even in the lions' den Daniel continued to pray and give thanks to God, knowing for a fact that his God was able to deliver him from the mouth of the lions.

So the first words that came out of Daniel's mouth did not curse the king; instead, his words brought a blessing to the king when he said, *"O king, live forever!"* He said that God had sent His angel and shut the lions' mouths. Daniel also said that he was innocent before God and had done no wrong to the king. What a place to be—innocent in the eyes of Almighty God and having done nothing wrong before the king.

Never, throughout the Scriptures, has it been a requirement for the saints of God to worship or to bow down before a man, even a king or world leader, placing him in a position that is not his to hold.

Daniel was delivered from the lions. Daniel's God—*our God*—was able to deliver him without injury being done to him in any way. In verse 23 we find the key to Daniel's success in surviving the night spent with the lions: *"He believed in his God."*

Do you believe in your God? Would you have lived to tell the story or would you have been the lions' midnight snack? I believe that, like Daniel, we must believe in our God! It is easy to *say* that we believe in our God, but do our actions speak louder than our words? In our believing are we going to God to bring about change into the lives of our kings, the ones who are in authority over us?

Are we like Daniel, continually serving our God? Or do we just run after God when trouble comes our way? Hebrews 11:6 says, *"He who comes to God must believe that He is, and that He is a rewarder of those who diligently seek Him."* In our believing we also must trust that He rewards those who diligently seek Him. Diligently seeking Him should be a continual part of our lives. It is not accomplished by just going to a church service once or twice a week. We are to *continually* serve God. There should be no stopping and starting in this. It is to be an ongoing part of our life.

The charge that we were given "first of all" in 1 Timothy has been in the past, is presently, and will also be in the future, a "first of all" requirement for the church to do in continually serving our God.

The Unchangeable Changed

Verse 24 in Daniel 6 goes on to say that after Daniel was released from the lions' den, the king gave another command. He commanded that all those men who had accused Daniel were to be brought, along with their wives and children, and cast into the lions' den. The lions destroyed them all.

When we pray, God goes to work on our behalf. Faith (believing) moves Him. He turned the whole thing around for Daniel; instead of Daniel being removed from the kingdom, all those conspirators who had opposed the laws of Daniel's God were removed. Their satanic plan backfired on them. It never was and it never will be a good idea to curse God or the people of God.

> *Then king Darius wrote unto all people, nations, and languages, that dwell in all the earth; Peace be multiplied unto you. I make a decree, That in every dominion of my kingdom men tremble and fear before the God of Daniel: for he is the living God, and stedfast for ever, and his kingdom*

that which shall not be destroyed, and his dominion shall be even unto the end. He delivereth and rescueth, and he worketh signs and wonders in heaven and in earth, who hath delivered Daniel from the power of the lions. So this Daniel prospered in the reign of Darius, and in the reign of Cyrus the Persian. Daniel 6:25-28 KJV

Can you see that even though the presidents and princes instigated a decree that attacked the law of God in that nation, that was not the conclusion of the matter? God was and is bigger than that. As I said previously, Daniel did not throw in the towel; even in the face of adversity he fell to his knees and took his requests, his petitions, before his God. He continued giving thanks to God. And even when they came and physically dragged him away, he did not back down.

I have heard it said that the Supreme Court decisions concerning prayer and Bible reading and the removal of the Ten Commandments from public places in the United States of America will never be changed. That's the same thing those presidents and princes of Medes and Persia thought. Even if there is some kind of "decree" or law in America that says once a ruling or decision has been made in our Supreme Court that it cannot be reconsidered or changed (which I have heard there is), that doesn't mean they won't be changed. That's what those men in Daniel's time found out!

If God did not exist, if there were no believers left to pray, then and only then would I think that *possibly* those Supreme Court decisions could not be changed. But, I believe that those decisions made in those former generations can become obsolete if we continue to do the things given us to do in "the charge":

Therefore I exhort first of all that supplications, prayers, intercessions, and giving of thanks be made for all men, for kings and all who are in authority, that we may lead a quiet and peaceable life in all godliness and reverence. 1 Timothy 2:1-2

The original decree of the presidents and princes was negated in the Persian empire when King Darius put into writing this statement to all peoples, nations and languages that dwell in all the earth, concerning the God of Daniel:

I make a decree that in every dominion of my kingdom men must tremble and fear before the God of Daniel. For He is the living God, and stedfast forever; and His kingdom is the one which shall not be destroyed, and His dominion shall endure to the end. He delivers and rescues, and He works signs and wonders in heaven and on earth, who has delivered Daniel from the power of the lions. Daniel 6:26-27

God is the living God. He delivers and rescues; He works signs and wonders in heaven and on earth. He delivered Daniel from the power of the lions.

Can your God deliver you? Can He rescue you? Can He deliver you from the power of the lions?

Can the church of Jesus Christ in this generation believe that our God can deliver us? Can the body of Christ in this generation believe that our God can rescue us from evil? Can we believe that our God can deliver us from the power of the lions?

If we can, then the unchangeable will change.

Chapter 12

A Generation That Sees Unreasonable and Wicked Rulers Stopped

Now about that time Herod the king stretched out his hand to harass some from the church. Then he killed James the brother of John with the sword. And because he saw that it pleased the Jews, he proceeded further to seize Peter also. Now it was during the Days of Unleavened Bread. So when he had arrested him, he put him in prison, and delivered him to four squads of soldiers to keep him, intending to bring him before the people after Passover. Peter was therefore kept in prison, but constant prayer was offered to God for him by the church. And when Herod was about to bring him out, that night Peter was sleeping, bound with two chains between two soldiers; and the guards before the door were keeping the prison. Now behold, an angel of the Lord stood by him, and a light shone in the prison;

and he struck Peter on the side and raised him up, saying, "Arise quickly!" And his chains fell off his hands. Then the angel said to him, "Gird yourself and tie on your sandals"; and so he did. And he said to him, "Put on your garment and follow me." So he went out and followed him, and did not know that what was done by the angel was real, but thought he was seeing a vision. When they were past the first and the second guard posts, they came to the iron gate that leads to the city, which opened to them of its own accord; and they went out and went down one street, and immediately the angel departed from him. And when Peter had come to himself, he said, "Now I know for certain that the Lord has sent His angel, and has delivered me from the hand of Herod and from all the expectation of the Jewish people." So, when he had considered this, he came to the house of Mary, the mother of John whose surname was Mark, where many were gathered together praying. And as Peter knocked at the door of the gate, a girl named Rhoda came to answer. When she recognized Peter's voice, because of her gladness she did not open the gate, but ran in and announced that Peter stood before the gate. But they said to her, "You are beside yourself!" Yet she kept insisting that it was so. So they said, "It is his angel." Now Peter continued knocking; and when they opened the door and saw him, they were astonished. But motioning to them with his hand to keep silent, he declared to them how the Lord had brought him out of the prison. And he said, "Go, tell these things to James and to the brethren." And he departed and went to another place. Acts 12:1-17

Herod the king was the latest successor in a line of ungodly kings who opposed the Christian faith. This Herod was the nephew of Herod Antipas, who had murdered John the Baptist, and was the grandson of Herod the Great. Herod the Great was the reigning king at the time of Christ's birth. When speaking with the wise men, he told them to come back to him after they found the Messiah and let him know where the child was so he could go and worship him. It was this same Herod who went on to murder all the male children in Bethlehem and its districts from the age of two years old and under, in his pursuit to kill the "newborn king."

At this point in time in Acts, Saul (Paul) had already come to know Jesus as his Lord, but the persecution against the church continued. Verse 1 of Acts 12 says that Herod the king began to harass some from the church and killed James, the brother of John, with the sword. James' martyrdom was the first murder of one of the original 12 disciples who had walked physically with the Lord.

Verse 3 goes on to say that since Herod's killing of the apostle James *"pleased the Jews,"* he decided to pursue taking Peter's life as well.

Our Father and God is very much aware of what is going on in every situation, especially when it involves His children, His church, being persecuted. Jesus takes this personally. Do you remember how Jesus asked Saul, *"Why are you persecuting Me?"* (Acts 9:4)

If you search through the New Testament Scriptures, you will find that after Herod took James' life, there are no more references to any of the other apostles being snatched away by this king or anyone else on some kind of crusade against God's people.

Before Herod could stop what Peter was doing in the kingdom of God, something big, something drastic, happened that changed Herod's whole plan.

The Church Went to War!

The church went to war! But it wasn't with physical weapons of war—it was with spiritual weapons. They did exactly what Paul later said in his letter to Timothy in "the charge" that the church should do "first of all" concerning all men and all those who are in authority. They prayed for both the apostle Peter and the "harassing" King Herod!

In Acts 12:5 it says that the church went to prayer without ceasing unto God for Peter. My King James Bible says, *"but prayer (*instant and earnest prayer) *was made without ceasing of the church unto God for him.*" James had been taken from them and now Peter was in danger of being removed from the church at Jerusalem. What was the difference between the two situations?

Maybe Satan told those Christians in the church at that time the lie that God, for some reason or another, needed James in Heaven. If you will study or *"be diligent to present yourself approved to God, a worker who does not need to be ashamed, rightly dividing the word of truth"* (2 Timothy 2:15), you will discover that such ideas are not of God. God needs us as His ambassadors right here on earth! Speaking of the value of people, the Scriptures say "*Precious in the sight of the Lord is the death of His saints"* (Psalm 117:115), and of the poor and needy, *"He shall spare the poor and needy...he shall redeem their soul from deceit and violence: and precious shall their blood be in his sight"* (Psalm 72:13-14 KJV). Every single saint of God is precious to Him and they are needed here more than they are needed in Heaven.

The apostle Paul had this to say concerning himself, Silvanus (Silas) and Timothy, who all were leaders in the body of Christ around A.D. 51 or 52:

> *Finally, brethren, pray for us, that the word of the Lord may run swiftly and be glorified, just as it is with you, and that we may be delivered from unreasonable and wicked men; for not all have faith. But the Lord is faithful, who will establish you and guard you from the evil one. And we have confidence in the Lord concerning you, both that you do and will do the things we command you.* 2 Thessalonians 3:1-4

What I see in the writings of the apostle Paul is that he had such a concern for the saints of God that he was always praying for them and their well-being. As he said in this passage, *"the Lord is faithful, who will establish you and guard you from the evil one"*!

Paul regularly requested that the saints continually pray for him as he prayed for them. The principle of giving and having it given back to you works in prayer. Give prayer and prayer will be given back to you. Sow prayer in the lives of others and you will reap back others praying for you.

Once again Paul spoke of the things that he wrote to the Thessalonians as *"things we command you"* (2 Thessalonians 3:4). He knew that he needed God to protect him from the evil in this world. He knew the power of prayer. He *commanded* them to pray for himself, Silas and Timothy, that they would be delivered from *"unreasonable and wicked men."*

Our Lord Jesus said this about what will happen when we agree together in prayer:

> *Assuredly, I say to you, whatever you bind on earth will be bound in heaven, and whatever you loose on earth will be loosed in heaven. Again I say to you that if two of you agree on earth concerning anything that they ask, it will be done for them by My Father in heaven. For where two or three are gathered together in My name, I am there in the midst of them.* Matthew 18:18-20

It is time for the saints of God to do by faith what we have been told to do in the Word of God. Do not hesitate when you see the enemy advancing against us; pray! In fact, even before we see any advancement of the enemy we need to pray. We are to pray without ceasing! I can't help but wonder if maybe the saints in Jerusalem were caught off guard in the beginning. Possibly they were not actually praying for the spiritual authorities or leaders in the church as they should have been when Satan, using Herod, stole the life and the ministry of James by killing him.

Jesus said that the thief—Satan, using men—comes to kill, to steal and to destroy (John 10:10).

God did not kill James. God does not violate His own commandments. One of those commandments is, *"You shall not murder"* (Exodus 20:13). *Herod* killed James. Did God allow it to happen? Obviously He did not stop it. But when the church—the body of Christ—began to pray, things changed.

While the church prayed, an angel of the Lord came to rescue Peter! A light shone in the prison when the angel appeared. The chains that bound him simply fell off his hands.

The Bible says that Peter didn't know that what was happening was real; he thought he was seeing a vision. Maybe Peter wasn't sure God was on the way. "This is too good to be true," could have been Peter's first thought. Nevertheless, every instruction that the angel of God gave him, Peter did. All the guards, including the two soldiers whom Peter had been chained between, did not respond against Peter and the angel. Apparently all the guards were supernaturally apprehended by the power of God. Even the iron gate *"opened to them of its own accord,"* as Peter, with the angel, escaped the prison Herod had placed him in.

When the angel departed and Peter had *"come to himself,"* he said, *"Now I know for certain that the Lord has sent His angel, and has delivered me from the hand of Herod and from all the expectation of the Jewish people."* (Actually, this was not Peter's first time to be supernaturally rescued from prison. Earlier, in Acts 5, Peter and some other apostles were delivered from prison by an angel of the Lord bringing them out.)

Before we go any further, I want to ask you one question: Do you know for certain that the Lord can send His angel and deliver you? Like the question King Darius asked Daniel, "Is the God that you continually serve able to deliver you?"

Church, do we believe that God can deliver us from the hand of our enemies? Do we believe that God's Word is true?

It is time we believe that our God—the most powerful, the Almighty God—*can* and *will* deliver and rescue those who trust in and call upon Him in times of trouble.

God calls Himself *El Shaddai* (*more than enough*), not *El Cheapo.* And when it comes to His awesome power, over and over the Bible calls Him the *Almighty God* (56 times throughout the Bible), not the *Almightless.*

Psalm 91:1 says, *"He who dwells in the secret place of the Most High shall abide under the shadow of the Almighty."* This is a very safe place to be! The psalmist went on in verse 2 to say, *"I will say of the LORD 'He is my refuge and my fortress; my God, in Him I will trust.'* "

Is He your "Almighty"? Can you say that the Lord is your refuge and your fortress? Are you dwelling in Him? There is only one safe place to dwell—and that is in Him!

Finding himself outside the prison, Peter went to the house of Mary, the mother of John, where the Scripture says *"many were gathered together praying,"* and they were *still* praying for him. Even though these people had been in constant prayer for Peter, when their prayers were answered and Peter was miraculously delivered, they couldn't comprehend it. That girl named Rhoda sure had a testimony to tell! She had been so excited at Peter's appearance, but then her fellow Christians told her that she was beside herself! And even after continuing to tell them that Peter was outside, they simply said that whoever she had seen at the gate must have been his angel!

When they said, *"It is his angel,"* it meant either that the manifestation of angels was a common occurrence or that they thought Peter had been killed and an angel or spirit had come to break the bad news to them. Meanwhile Peter was patiently waiting outside, knocking. When the saints finally saw Peter, they were astonished.

These people were very much like many Christians today. When God answers our prayers, we can hardly believe it happened. Yet, when we begin to pray in faith, according to the Word of God and His will, God responds, He hears, He helps, He answers. We need to expect the things we desire of Him in prayer to come to pass.

I believe that this event changed the lives of all those involved in the church, as well as Peter's. It was an event that strengthened them in their faith in a time of desperation. And I am sure that Peter once again had confidence, knowing that an angel had delivered him when otherwise he was heading for certain death.

Herod: A King Who Did Not Give Glory to God

> *Then, as soon as it was day, there was no small stir among the soldiers about what had become of Peter. But when Herod had searched for him and not found him, he examined the guards and commanded that they should be put to death. And he went down from Judea to Caesarea, and stayed there. Now Herod had been very angry with the people of Tyre and Sidon; but they came to him with one accord, and having made Blastus the king's personal aide their friend, they asked for peace, because their country was supplied with food by the king's country. So on a set day Herod, arrayed in royal apparel, sat on his throne and gave an oration to them. And the people kept shouting, "The voice of a god and not of a man!" Then immediately an angel of the Lord struck him, because he did not give glory to God. And he was eaten by worms and died. But the word of God grew and multiplied. And Barnabas and Saul returned from Jerusalem when they had fulfilled their ministry, and they also took with them John whose surname was Mark.* Acts 12:18-25

This story about Peter and Herod in Acts is very similar to that of Daniel in the lions' den. In the first place, Herod was not very happy that Peter had vanished, for that meant the Jews were not going to be as pleased as Herod had hoped to make them. Apparently the angel of the Lord had put all the guards to sleep so they did not realize until morning that Peter had somehow mysteriously escaped from the prison. So similar to the actions King Darius took, Herod commanded that all the guards be put to death.

When Daniel, and now in this setting Peter, were preserved from destruction, Satan, whom Jesus calls a *"murderer from the beginning"* (John 8:44), was angered and brought about death, or murder, to others. Satan is very ruthless; it is best if we remain in that safe place in Christ.

Unlike King Darius, Herod did not see or recognize that there was someone at work here helping Peter, that God had rescued him from the wrath of his hand. Herod was an angry man; the Bible says he was already angry with the people of Tyre and Sidon.

All in all, Herod was not doing a very good job of serving as a king. Eventually Herod let his kingship go to his head. He rejected the fact that he was not a god and when the people proclaimed in their shouting that his was *"the voice of a god and not of a man,"* an angel of the Lord struck him. He died because *"he did not give glory to God."* The Scripture explicitly says that Herod *"was eaten by worms and died."*

I believe that this Herod, along with his predecessors, had plenty of time to repent and turn to the living God, to acknowledge the lordship of Jesus Christ and to submit themselves to His authority, but they would not.

It is God's will that all men be saved, including all the kings and rulers of the earth. Once again Jesus had to stop the abuse of a man in a position of authority. God is not a child abuser; He does not abuse His children. Neither will He allow man to continue to abuse God's people in this manner. In a way such men are fighting against God Himself, as Saul was doing. I believe that Herod *could have* come to a place of repentance like any other man or woman.

When the church of the Lord Jesus Christ prayed according to "the charge" given to it, the man whom God was using was released. The man whom Satan was using was stopped. Herod did not give glory to God; instead, he chose to take to himself what belonged only to God. This was his fatal mistake. Herod was stopped, and Acts 12:24 says the Word of God grew and multiplied.

When "the charge" is carried out—when supplications, prayers, intercessions and giving of thanks are made for all men, for kings and all who are in authority—then the church of Jesus Christ will lead a quiet and peaceable life in all godliness and reverence. *"For this is good and acceptable in the sight of God our Savior, who desires all men to be saved and to come to the knowledge of the truth"* (1 Timothy 2:3-4)!

God once again sent His angel! The life of God's man was preserved. The work of Satan against the church was stopped. A king who opposed what God desired for His people was struck by the angel of our Lord and died. God's will prevailed. The Word of God grew and spread throughout the land!

Can we believe that God can do this now, in this generation? I think that He can.

PART IV

For All Who Are in Authority

Chapter 13

A Generation That Prays for "Worst-Case Scenarios"

When you read the book of Acts, you read a lot about a man once named Saul. Many referred to him as Saul of Tarsus. This man had a bad reputation among the Christians. He was known for hanging out at the stoning (murder, using big rocks!) of Christians by angry mobs in his spare time as a young person (read Acts 7:58). Then he graduated from just attending those type of events to actually being the man with the authority from local leaders to seek out Christians and have them killed.

It was written of this man Saul that he *"made havoc of the church, entering every house, and dragging off men and women, committing them to prison"* (Acts 8:3). This fellow must have had some kind of mad, psychotic, demon-driven desire to inflict such punishment on people who were not hurting anyone, but simply trying their best to be "Christians." It also was written that Saul breathed *"threats and murder against the disciples of the Lord"* (Acts 9:1).

Saul seemed to have one goal: Find men and women who were serving and preaching Jesus and have them bound and brought to the officials to be imprisoned or killed. Later on, Saul is quoted as saying,

> *Indeed, I myself thought I must do many things contrary to the name of Jesus of Nazareth....and many of the saints I shut up in prison, having received authority...and when they were put to death, I cast my vote against them. And I punished them often...and being exceedingly enraged against them, I persecuted them even to foreign cities.* Acts 26:9-11

How would you like to have had a guy like that for a neighbor? This man had to have been demon-driven; we might even have called him "Satan's right-hand man" at the time. How often would you have "happy thoughts" about a man such as this Saul? If you are not familiar with the story I just presented, I encourage you to read the book of Acts in the Bible.

Before we look again at what happened to this Saul, I want to ask you, "If you were one of those Christians, what would you have been doing? What would you have been saying about this madman possibly dragging you off to prison to be martyred, killed for being a disciple of Jesus of Nazareth?"

Do you remember the "charge" given to us "first of all"?

Saul was not in just the *"all men"* category of the command; he also was in the *"all who are in authority"* section! We must be making prayers, supplications, intercessions and giving of thanks even when things are not going the way we hope they would!

Here's the exciting news: The Saul whom we have been describing as persecutor of the church is the very Paul we have been quoting! He is the one who, by the Holy Spirit, gave the "charge" to Timothy, to the church and to us as readers of God's Word today.

However, during the first century A.D., Saul was persecuting all the Christians in and around the city of Jerusalem. The officials who gave him the authority to do so were the Hebrew leaders in the highest ranked positions, including the high priest at Jerusalem. Saul was working for this group trying to bring an end to the Christian faith.

This is what happens when truth is rejected in a generation. The very ones whom Jesus came to save, grow up to murder and persecute Christians.

Think about it. More than likely these same officials were the children or grandchildren of the folks who saw and heard of Jesus face to face as He went about in His mission here on the earth, even dying on the cross in the very city of Jerusalem.

I'm sure that everything was going along great for these officials until one day Saul went on a trip to Damascus. He was headed there *"with authority and commission from the chief priests"* (Acts 26:12) to round up more Christians. It was more than 150 miles from Jerusalem to Damascus, which means it was probably a lot of work to journey there just to bring in more Christians. Everything was fine, until...

Stopped in His Tracks

Right in the middle of Saul's commission, something happened that changed him forever. This is the way Paul explained the life-changing event that took place when Jesus Himself showed up to stop the man in his tracks. This is Paul's own account, as recorded in Acts 26:12-18, when he shared his testimony before King Agrippa:

> *While thus occupied, as I journeyed to Damascus with authority and commission from the chief priests, at midday, O king, along the road I saw a light from heaven, brighter than the sun, shining around me and those who journeyed with me. And when we all had fallen to the ground, I heard a voice speaking to me and saying in the Hebrew language, "Saul, Saul, why are you persecuting Me? It is hard for you to kick against the goads." So I said, "Who are You, Lord?" And He said, "I am Jesus, whom you are persecuting. But rise and stand on your feet; for I have appeared to you for this purpose, to make you a minister and a witness both of the things which you have seen and of the things which I will yet reveal to you. I will deliver you from the Jewish people, as well as from the Gentiles, to whom I now send you, to open their eyes, in order to turn them from darkness to light, and from the power of Satan to God, that they may receive*

forgiveness of sins and an inheritance among those who are sanctified by faith in Me."

Did you notice that the way Jesus saw it, Saul was persecuting *Him* by persecuting the church? And Jesus was bringing an end to it.

Where most Bibles use the words *"it is hard for you to kick against the goads"* or as the King James Versions says it, *"pricks,"* the New Living Translation puts it this way: *"It is hard for you to fight against my will."* This is how Paul's conversion to Christianity came about. All along he thought that, as a Hebrew, he was helping God by stopping the Christians from continuing to express and pursue their faith in Jesus. Even the religious leaders at Jerusalem, the chief priests and the high priest, really believed that they were serving God by stamping out Christianity.

Once again, God does not do things the way we would probably do them. He does things His way. He's allowed to do that—He is God!

Do you think that those persecuted Christians were praying for Saul? Do you think that they were possibly giving thanks to God whenever his name came to their minds? I believe that they were praying for him. I also believe that they were making supplications and intercessions for him as well. I even believe that they were giving thanks to God for this man. (Later on we will look at ways that we can do this in our lives.)

Do you remember that it also is God's will that all men be saved, even Saul? God's will came to pass in his life even though he was far from it and "kicking" against it. He was in actuality fighting against God, fighting against the truth—Jesus Himself. He was a worst-case scenario, yet God saved him!

Do you presently know anyone like this? Do you know of anyone in positions of authority who compare to Saul? Many would have said he was "bad to the bone," a "bad dude," a killer, a flat-out murderer of innocent people! He was acting as an enemy of Jesus because he was deceived, but he got saved! He "saw the light" brighter than the sun. That light brought Saul and his companions to the ground. He literally had a blinding experience; when he stood to his feet he couldn't see, for he was blind. He went without sight for three days.

Acts 9:10-19 describes what happened next:

Now there was a certain disciple at Damascus named Ananias; and to him the Lord said in a vision, "Ananias." And he said, "Here I am, Lord." So the Lord said to him, "Arise and go to the street called Straight, and inquire at the house of Judas for one called Saul of Tarsus, for behold, he is praying. And in a vision he has seen a man named Ananias coming in and putting his hand on him, so that he might receive his sight." Then Ananias answered, "Lord, I have heard from many about this man, how much harm he has done to Your saints in Jerusalem. And here he has authority from the chief priests to bind all who call on Your name." But the Lord said to him, "Go, for he is a chosen vessel of Mine to bear My name before Gentiles, kings, and the children of Israel. For I will show him how many things he must suffer for My name's sake." And Ananias went his way and entered the house; and laying his hands on him he said, "Brother Saul, the Lord Jesus, who appeared to you on the road as you came, has sent me that you may receive your sight and be filled with the Holy Spirit." Immediately there fell from his eyes something like scales, and he received his sight at once; and he arose and was baptized. So when he had received food, he was strengthened. Then Saul spent some days with the disciples at Damascus.

The Role of Ananias

One of the disciples of the Lord, a man named Ananias, probably one of the very ones whom Saul might have imprisoned or even put to death if things had continued to go as they were, ended up being the one to pray for Saul. This "unknown" man of God was used by God to heal Saul's eyes and to cause Saul to be filled with the Holy Spirit and then water baptized.

Ananias simply did what it takes to be used by the Lord. He said, "Here am I, Lord," and then he did what the Lord asked him to do, which was lay his hands on Saul and pray for him. When he did, he saw him changed by the power of God.

By the way, Ananias was not one of the original 12 disciples; he wasn't some superhero whom everyone in the church knew about. He was simply, as the Bible calls him, *"a certain disciple"* who had a vision and responded the correct way to the voice of Jesus when called upon.

Look at Acts 2:17-18:

> *And it shall come to pass in the last days, says God, that I will pour out of My Spirit on all flesh; your sons and your daughters shall prophesy, your young men shall see visions, your old men shall dream dreams. And on My menservants and on My maidservants I will pour out My Spirit in those days, and they shall prophesy.*

If you are a believer in the Lord Jesus Christ, God wants to pour out His Spirit on you in our time. The *"last days"* began on the Day of Pentecost, which occurred 50 days after Jesus' resurrection from the grave. Pentecost was a festival the Jews had celebrated for thousands of years. It was one of those many shadows of things to come (Colossians 2:16-17). Its symbolism was completed when, as Acts 2:1 says, *"the Day of Pentecost had fully come."* The Holy Spirit, as promised by Jesus Himself (Acts 1:4-8), came upon the Christians in the upper room to empower them to be witnesses in this world.

Ananias was a "charismatic" Christian. (The Charismatic Movement of today is not a new thing.) He was just one of the many sons and daughters whom God said shall prophesy. He was a man who walked in the promise that the young men would see visions. All who were waiting on the promise of the Holy Spirit's coming were filled with the Holy Spirit on the Day of Pentecost. Along with the 11 disciples, there were both men and women, Mary the mother of Jesus and Jesus' earthly born brothers. All together about 120 people were there in the initial outpouring of the Holy Spirit (Acts 1:14-15). Since that Day of Pentecost, the Holy Spirit has continued on the earth, working in and through all who would receive Him and His power to spread the message of the Gospel of Jesus Christ. He has given to us His power to be witnesses to Him in our Jerusalems, Judeas and Samarias and to the end of the earth.

This was God's plan to take the Gospel from its consummation at Jerusalem, which included Jesus' death, burial and resurrection and the outpouring of the Spirit, to the surrounding cities and then from there to all the earth.

The Men Standing By

Paul's conversion is related in three different places in the book of Acts. The first account of it was narrated by the writer of Acts, believed to be Luke, who wrote to a man named Theophilus (see Luke 1:1 and Acts 1:1). In Luke's second person telling of Paul's conversion in Acts 9:1-9, he wrote about it like this:

> *Then Saul, still breathing threats and murder against the disciples of the Lord, went to the high priest and asked letters from him to the synagogues of Damascus, so that if he found any who were of the Way, whether men or women, he might bring them bound to Jerusalem. As he journeyed he came near Damascus, and suddenly a light shone around him from heaven. Then he fell to the ground, and heard a voice saying to him, "Saul, Saul, why are you persecuting Me?" And he said, "Who are You, Lord?" Then the Lord said, "I am Jesus, whom you are persecuting. It is hard for you to kick against the goads." So he, trembling and astonished, said, "Lord, what do You want me to do?" Then the Lord said to him, "Arise and go into the city, and you will be told what you must do." And the men who journeyed with him stood speechless, hearing a voice but seeing no one. Then Saul arose from the ground, and when his eyes were opened he saw no one. But they led him by the hand and brought him into Damascus. And he was three days without sight, and neither ate nor drank.*

In verse 5, Saul's first response was, *"Who are You, Lord?"* While trembling, he then asked, *"Lord, what do You want me to do?"* The Lord responded by saying, *"Arise and go into the city, and you will be told what you must do"* (verse 6).

As a result of the Lord's appearing, Saul's plans were completely turned around. This was quite a humbling time for such a man as him.

This account says in verse 7 that *"the men who journeyed with him stood speechless, hearing a voice but seeing no one."* In the third account of Saul's conversion, found in Acts 22:9, Paul said, *"Those who were with me indeed saw the light, and were afraid, but they did not hear the voice of Him who spoke to me."* This is not a contradiction. I believe that what happened was that the men did indeed hear a voice but did not comprehend what that voice was saying directly to Saul. Only Saul received the instruction from Jesus Himself.

Have you ever noticed that when God shows up physically in His glory, men fall to the ground? And if they do not know Him, they tremble and are afraid. Our God is an awesome God!

Praying for All Men—Including Saul

In Acts 9:12, the Lord told Ananias that Saul *"in a vision...has seen a man named Ananias coming in and putting his hand on him, so that he might receive his sight."*

God knows all; He knows the end from the beginning; there is nothing unknown to Him. Before it actually happened, the Holy Spirit showed Saul Ananias's coming to him. The Holy Spirit also knew exactly where Saul was and what he was doing.

Ananias knew from the things he had heard about Saul that he had done much harm to the saints in Jerusalem and that he had authority from the chief priests to bind all who call on the name of the Lord. This is the way Saul was known by men.

But the Lord saw Saul differently. Jesus saw him as a *"chosen vessel"* who would bear His name before Gentiles, kings and the children of Israel (see Acts 9:15).

If Ananias had continued to see Saul by what he knew about him, he probably would not have gone out of his way to find this Saul of Tarsus. But through the "vision," through seeing things through the eyes of God, he could see that this man, despite his reputation, was a *chosen vessel* of Jesus.

Saul all along was just a man whom God desired to save and come into the knowledge of the truth.

The Bible does not say this, but I believe that someday we might find out that Ananias was praying for and making supplications and intercessions and giving of thanks for the man Saul. Maybe he did it either knowingly or unknowingly by praying in the Holy Spirit, while Saul was in a position of authority.

We are not to pray only for the good guys; we are to go beyond that into a realm of faith where our obedience to God's Word extends beyond all that we know and experience in the realm of our senses. Could Ananias have been praying for Saul that God would stop what he was doing and bring truth to him, that he would be saved and be used by Jesus with the same zeal to proclaim Jesus as the Christ and the way to God? Could it be possible that Ananias, during his time of worship and praise, was thanking God that despite all he had heard, this Saul could one day be a chosen vessel in the kingdom of God? I believe that *someone* was praying for him.

There is one more thing I want you to see here concerning Ananias and his ministering to Saul.

Jesus is in the business of using men and women to carry out His will in this earth. He could have physically showed up again to Saul after three days, but instead He got a man involved in His plan for Saul's life. He sent Ananias this time to lay his hands on Saul, that he might be healed and filled with the Holy Spirit.

Would you have laid your hands on Saul and prayed for him, or would you have laid your hands on him to strangle him? Is there a Saul in your world today? What are you doing about him? What are you saying about him?

Remember, it is not a man or woman who truly is your enemy. An unseen world full of spirits is influencing mankind. At times they control mankind. We need to see and recognize who the real enemy is.

In Acts 9:20-21, the Bible says this about Paul's transformation after his deliverance as a tool in Satan's use:

> *Immediately he preached the Christ in the synagogues, that He is the Son of God. Then all who heard were amazed, and said, "Is this not he who destroyed those who called on this name in Jerusalem, and has come here for that purpose, so that he might bring them bound to the chief priests?"*

God saved a worst-case scenario named Saul. Our God can save those who seem to be worst-case scenarios today! All we need to do is fulfill the charge.

Chapter 14

A Generation That Prays for Leaders in the Church

Therefore I exhort first of all that supplications, prayers, intercessions, and giving of thanks be made for all men, for kings and all who are in authority.... 1 Timothy 2:1-2

Brethren, pray for us [Paul, Silvanus and Timothy]. 1 Thessalonians 5:25

Pray for us [the writer of Hebrews and those with him at Italy]... Hebrews 13:18

Praying always...for all the saints—and for me [Paul]... Ephesians 6:18-19

Even though the apostle Paul was a great man of faith and power and greatly used by God to take the Gospel of Jesus Christ through Asia and Europe and eventually the whole world through his writings, he needed the saints of God to pray for him.

As you can see from these passages, all believed to have been written by Paul's own hand (or dictated to an assistant), Paul was counting on the prayers of the churches to help him fulfill God's purposes. He was well aware of the importance of making supplications, prayers, intercessions and giving of thanks for all men.

The apostle Paul was not a hypocrite; he didn't tell us to do one thing and then himself go and do something different. It is evident in his writings that he was indeed praying and carrying out "the charge" himself.

Whether you realize it or not, leaders in the church are human too. Every one of them eats, sleeps and "puts his pants on one leg at a time," just like you do. They are not super-human or super-spiritual beings on some higher spiritual plane than the one you are on. They need you to pray for them.

And if you don't believe that you yourself need the prayers of the saints, you had better think again. In the very next chapter following the charge given to us "first of all," Paul said that being puffed up with pride will cause a man to fall into the same condemnation as the devil (1 Timothy 3:6). Also, Proverbs 16:18 says, *"Pride goes before destruction, and a haughty spirit before a fall."*

It is a dangerous place to be in when you think you do not need anyone else to pray for you. I can guarantee you that you are not wiser than the apostle Paul, who wrote more than half of the New Testament Scriptures by the Holy Spirit's inspiration. For Paul, as a leader in the church, needed to be refreshed, strengthened and encouraged just like any other believer.

For example, look in the book of Philemon, where Paul wrote to his friend Philemon as well as to Apphia and Archippus, the pastors of the church in his house at Colosse. In his request to come to stay with them he wrote,

> *Yes, brother, let me have joy from you in the Lord; refresh my heart in the Lord. Having confidence in your obedience, I write to you, knowing that you will do even more than I say. But, meanwhile, also prepare a guest room for me, for I trust that through your prayers I shall be granted to you.*
> Philemon 1:20-22

Strive Together With Me in Prayer

Not only did Paul need times of refreshing personally, but he also believed that the power in the prayers of others would join with his own before God.

In Romans 15:29-32 he wrote these words:

> *But I know that when I come to you, I shall come in the fullness of the blessing of the gospel of Christ. Now I beg you, brethren, through the Lord Jesus Christ, and through the love of the Spirit, that you strive together with me in your prayers to God for me, that I may be delivered from those in Judea who do not believe, and that my service for Jerusalem may be acceptable to the saints, that I may come to you with joy by the will of God, and may be refreshed together with you.*

Again in this time in Paul's life, he was going to Rome to be "refreshed" together with them. Paul needed to go to Rome *"in the fullness of the blessing"* of the Gospel of Christ; he did not want to go in part of or in half of the blessing.; He wanted to be in the fullness of it. It appears that he needed his brethren to pray to God for him for this fullness to come about. He asked them to strive together with him in their prayers to God. He said that in doing this, he could be delivered from those in Judea who might try to prevent him from completing his journey to Jerusalem.

Pray That the Word of the Lord May Have Free Course

As we have been seeing over and over again, Paul and other well-known (in their day) men of God needed the prayers of the saints.

Paul, with Silvanus (Silas) and Timothy, when writing to the church at Thessalonica, wrote, *"Finally, brethren, pray for us, that the word of the Lord may run swiftly* [KJV, have free course] *and be glorified, just as it is with you, and that we may be delivered from unreasonable and wicked men; for not all have faith"* (2 Thessalonians 3:1-2).

You would think that Paul, having Silas and Timothy with him, would not need the prayers of anyone else, right? Wrong. They, like any other child of

God, knew that the way to get God's blessing was to do things God's way. Obedience to God's Word always brings about blessing.

These preachers of the Gospel needed the saints in the church to pray for them that God's Word would be preached, have free course and not be prevented by the unreasonable and wicked men Satan would use to try to hinder it.

These same three men went on to say, *"But the Lord is faithful, who will establish you and guard you from the evil one. And we have confidence in the Lord concerning you, both that you do and will do the things we command you"* (2 Thessalonians 3:3-4).

Sounds like the fulfillment of the charge coming to pass in the earth, doesn't it? The saints praying for the church leaders, and the church leaders praying for and speaking a blessing over the saints of God. The Word of God being preached with free course, without opposition; the people of God being established and guarded from the evil one; and God's men being protected as well. Sounds like a quiet and peaceable life in all reverence and godliness coming to pass on the earth.

Stand With Me

In 2 Timothy 4:16-18, as a testimony to the power of God working in his life, Paul wrote:

> *At my first defense no one stood with me, but all forsook me. May it not be charged against them. But the Lord stood with me and strengthened me, so that the message might be preached fully through me, and that all the Gentiles might hear. And I was delivered out of the mouth of the lion. And the Lord will deliver me from every evil work and preserve me for His heavenly kingdom. To Him be glory forever and ever. Amen!*

The apostle Paul needed others to stand with him. Fortunately, when there were times that no one could be found, Jesus was there and stood with Paul and strengthened him. In Paul's own words, it was *"so that the message might be fully preached through me, and all the Gentiles might hear."*

Paul went on and said that he was delivered out of the mouth of the lion! As we saw in Chapter 11, Daniel also was delivered out of the mouth of the lion because he believed in his God. Paul believed in his God and he was delivered from the one who goes about like a roaring lion—Satan.

Paul's confession was, *"And the Lord will deliver me from every evil work and preserve me for His heavenly kingdom."* There is power in praying together in agreement for deliverance and protection from Satan and those he would use to prevent the Good News from being proclaimed in the earth.

Pray for Me, That I May Speak Boldly

> *Praying always...for all saints—and for me, that utterance may be given to me, that I may open my mouth boldly to make known the mystery of the gospel, for which I am an ambassador in chains; that in it I may speak boldly, as I ought to speak.* Ephesians 6:18-20

When Paul instructed us on how to complete the putting on of the whole armor of God by praying always in the Spirit for all saints, he wanted to be included in their prayers. He wanted the armor-bearing saints of God to pray for him. He wanted prayer so that utterance would be given to him from God (divine inspiration from the Father). He wanted prayer to be bold in his preaching in making known the mystery of the Gospel, which is Christ in us. He wanted prayer so that he could boldly speak the things that the Lord was asking of him to speak.

The apostle Paul truly was a Godly leader; he was a man of power as well as a man of Godly humility. He set forth an example for all Christian leaders to take note of.

Saints of God, you who are armored saints of God, you and I need to be praying for the apostles, prophets, evangelists, pastors and teachers God has placed in the body of Christ in this age, in our generation.

Concerning ministry gifts in the church, Peter wrote,

> *As each one has received a gift, minister it to one another, as good stewards of the manifold grace of God. If anyone speaks, let him speak as the*

> *oracles of God. If anyone ministers, let him do it as with the ability which God supplies, that in all things God may be glorified through Jesus Christ, to whom belong the glory and the dominion forever and ever. Amen.* 1 Peter 4:10-11

We need to pray for those who are ministers, that they would be good stewards of the gift God has given to them and that God by His Holy Spirit would enable them to speak for God as His oracle or as His voice in the church. Also, we should pray that they would do it not in their own ability, but in the ability God has given them.

The End of All Things

Just before the apostle Peter wrote these Scriptures about the oracle gifts, he told the church,

> *But the end of all things is at hand; therefore be serious and watchful in your prayers. And above all things have fervent love for one another, for "love will cover a multitude of sins." Be hospitable to one another without grumbling.* 1 Peter 4:7-9

Can we in this generation be the church of Jesus Christ that is serious, or sober, as the King James Version says, and watchful in our prayers? The Word of God is true; the end of all things is near! It is time for us to have fervent love for one another. It is time to stop exploiting one another's sins and let the love of God cover a multitude of sins. In case you haven't discovered it by now, there is only one who is sinless; and thanks be to God for Him—Jesus!

It is like the situation when the adulterous woman was brought before the Lord during His earthly ministry. He told those who wanted to kill her for her sin, *"He who is without sin among you, let him throw a stone at her first"* (John 8:7). All the men who had found her guilty of sin left one by one, without throwing a stone, until there was none left with her but Jesus alone. Apparently they all were guilty of some kind of sin in their own lives—all of them except for the Sinless One who would be the sacrifice for the sin debt of all of mankind, Jesus, the Lamb of God. There is no one living now or before us or after us who is sinless, except for our Savior!

We must be serious and watchful in our prayers. Above all we must have fervent love for one another. And finally, we need to be hospitable to one another without grumbling.

These are not just good suggestions found in the Word of God; they are not optional to a Christian lifestyle. These are New Testament commands given to the church by the Holy Spirit of God. The last command is certainly not the least. Whether you are a leader or not, be hospitable to one another and quit the grumbling. If you don't know what it means to be "hospitable," please look it up in your dictionary. The world without Christ has a "dog eat dog" mind-set, but the saints of the Most High God need to have a "love one another" mind-set.

I am praying that God will cause us to be serious and watchful in our prayers, that the body of Christ would be fervent in love for one another and that the saints of God would be hospitable toward all.

It is time for the post-Sunday morning service lunches of "roasted pastor" to come to an end. Every time you think about any Christian leader or ministry gift God has placed in your life, thank God for them and pray for them in a way that is pleasing to the Father. I want to challenge you to pray in the Spirit for them when God puts them on your heart. War against the powers of darkness on their behalf. Choose to strive together with them in prayer and fight against our common enemy—the devil.

Remember the words of Peter: *"The end of all things is at hand."* Let's do God's Word that He commands. Together in prayer, we will fight, we will win, we will overcome!

Chapter 15

Could This Be the Church's Finest Hour?

Then the multitude rose up together against them [Paul and Silas]*; and the magistrates tore off their clothes and commanded them to be beaten with rods. And when they had laid many stripes on them, they threw them into prison, commanding the jailer to keep them securely. Having received such a charge, he put them into the inner prison and fastened their feet in the stocks. But at midnight Paul and Silas were praying and singing hymns to God, and the prisoners were listening to them. Suddenly there was a great earthquake, so that the foundations of the prison were shaken; and immediately all the doors were opened and everyone's chains were loosed. And the keeper of the prison, awaking from sleep and seeing the prison doors open, supposing the prisoners had fled, drew his sword and was about to kill himself. But Paul called with a loud voice, saying, "Do yourself no harm, for we are all here." Then he called for a light, ran in,* *and fell down trembling before Paul and Silas. And he brought them out and said, "Sirs, what must I do to be saved?" So they said, "Believe on the Lord Jesus Christ, and you will be saved, you and your household." Then they spoke the word of the Lord to him and to all who were in his house. And he took them the same hour of the night and washed their stripes. And immediately he and all his family were baptized. Now when he had brought them into his house, he set food before them; and he rejoiced, having believed in God with all his household. And when it was day, the magistrates sent the officers, saying, "Let those men go." So the keeper of the prison reported these words to Paul, saying, "The magistrates have sent to let you go. Now therefore depart, and go in peace."* Acts 16:22-36

Normally you would think of people going to jail for things like murder, theft, etc. Here the apostle Paul and his ministry partner Silas were imprisoned for preaching the Gospel in the streets of Thyatira. These men were changing the lives of many in this city; people were getting saved, healed and delivered of demons. As usual, Satan was getting walloped by the Holy Spirit working in and through these men of God.

So what happened? Earlier Paul and Silas were being continually harassed by a slave girl who was possessed with a spirit of divination, which had *"brought her masters much profit by fortune-telling"* (Acts 16:16). She had been following Paul and his companions, including Luke, who wrote this account. She would cry out, saying, *"These men are the servants of the Most High God, who proclaim to us the way of salvation"* (verse 17). After many days of this Paul became *"greatly annoyed"* and commanded the spirit to come out of her, which it did *"that very hour"* (verse 18). (By the way, God doesn't need demons to help Him advertise!)

As a result, this girl's fortune-telling business came to an end. Her masters' money-making business was closed down. Her bosses weren't too happy about what Paul did to their business, so they dragged Paul and Silas into the marketplace to the authorities.

As a side note, notice that the Word of God says this "fortune-teller" was possessed with a demon spirit of divination. Don't be deceived by going to a fortune-teller to find out your future. Satan does not know anyone's future. But if he can get you to believe a story some psychic tells you, he will make sure you see it come to pass. Many people have been seduced by the information predicted by the devil himself. It is one of the many ways he deceives and keeps people from the truth that is found only in Jesus.

Leviticus 19:31 says, *"Give no regard to mediums and familiar spirits; do not seek after them, to be defiled by them: I am the LORD your God."* God calls all of Satan's counterfeit programs *"abominations"* in Deuteronomy 18:9-14. God does not want us going to fortune-tellers or psychics to find out our purpose in life; He wants us to find our direction by seeking after Him and hearing His Word. He says in Jeremiah 29:11, *"For I know the thoughts that I think toward you, says the LORD, thoughts of peace and not of evil, to give you a future and a hope."* His plan is for your best; Satan's plan is for your destruction.

So when Paul and Silas messed up their fortune-telling business, these men hauled them off to the authorities. Now by this time rumors were probably going around about these men of God, how Christians were vanishing from jails and escaping with supernatural help. Perhaps that is why the jailer received strict orders to keep them safe, and why he put them in the inner prison and their feet in stocks.

Here we see, though, that Paul practiced what he preached. Before he ever wrote of the charge to Timothy, I believe that Paul had learned throughout the years how to correctly respond to the adversity he encountered. When he exhorted, *"first of all that supplications, prayers, intercessions, and giving of thanks be made for all men, for kings and all who are in authority, that we may lead a quiet and peaceable life in all godliness and reverence,"* he was writing out of personal experience. He knew from his past situations and life events what to do to bring about a quiet and peaceable life in all godliness and reverence. He knew the way to bring all that to pass and he wrote it in his charge so we could know how to do it too.

Despite what people have done to you or might be about to do to you, remember this charge and do it!

Read through the book of Acts and you will see how Paul responded over and over again in a manner pleasing to God. As a result, God was always there in Paul's finest as well as darkest hours.

The Midnight Hour

One of those hours came in verse 25 of Acts 16. There the Bible says, *"At midnight Paul and Silas were praying and singing hymns to God, and the prisoners were listening to them."*

Paul and Silas could have been really bummed out about where they found themselves at the end of the day. Just when everything was going well with their preaching and ministering, here they were in the most undesirable place to be—prison. The jails of those days were not anything like the prisons we have here in America. This was not a place that would lift your spirit; this was not a happy place to be. These men could have been down in the dumps and thrown in the towel.

They could have sung, "Why me, Lord, what did I ever do…?" They could have complained to each other about how bad things were. They could have made all kinds of comments about those masters of that slave girl or the authorities who had misused their power by putting them in such a disgusting place. That is exactly what Satan would have liked them to do. They would have been feeling low and Satan would have been flying high. But that is not what the Holy Spirit would have Spirit-filled men do.

Instead, "the charge" went into action! Paul and Silas were praying and singing hymns to God at midnight. I believe that these men were making supplications, prayers, intercessions and giving of thanks for all men, for kings and all who are in authority. I believe that they were fulfilling "the charge" for the men who had dragged them off to the authorities; for the authorities who had sentenced them to prison; for the jailer who had locked them up; for the others there in the prison.

In their prayers they very well could have been thanking God for all the people I just listed. Knowing that it is God's will for all men to be saved and to come to the knowledge of the truth, they more than likely were thanking God for bringing all these men into their lives so that God could bring the Good News to all involved.

By the way, isn't Paul the one who wrote, *"We know that all things work together for good to those who love God, to those who are the called according to His purpose"* (Romans 8:28)? Can we begin to look for something good to happen when it seems like things are going bad? Yes, we can!

Not only were Paul and Silas praying, they also were singing! They were singing hymns to God! They were singing praises to God. They were probably singing from the Psalms. At the time of Christ, the hymn commonly used was the part of the "Hallel," which consisted of Psalms 113–118.[1]

They might have been singing lyrics like these:

Praise the LORD! Praise, O servants of the LORD, praise the name of the LORD! Blessed be the name of the LORD from this time forth and forevermore! From the rising of the sun to its going down the LORD's name is to be praised. Psalm 113:1-3

Or:

Not unto us, O LORD, not unto us, but to Your name give glory, because of Your mercy, because of Your truth. Why should the Gentiles say, "So where is their God?"... The LORD has been mindful of us; He will bless us; He will bless the house of Israel; He will bless the house of Aaron. He will bless those who fear the LORD, both small and great. Psalm 115:1-2,12-13

Or:

I love the LORD, because He has heard my voice and my supplications. Because He has inclined His ear to me, therefore I will call upon Him as long as I live. Psalm 116:1-2

Or:

The voice of rejoicing and salvation is in the tents of the righteous; the right hand of the LORD does valiantly. The right hand of the LORD is exalted; the right hand of the LORD does valiantly. I shall not die, but live, and declare the works of the LORD. Psalm 118:15-17

Or:

This is the day the LORD has made; we will rejoice and be glad in it. Psalm 118:24

The Hallel Psalms

Psalm 118, which is a psalm of declarative praise, is the climax of the group of psalms called the Passover Psalms, or Hallel Psalms, after the Hebrew word for praise.[2] This is where the word *hallelujah* comes from. These psalms, which include Psalms 113—118, were probably sung by the Lord Jesus on the night before His death (see Matthew 26:30; Mark 14:26). It also is a strong possibility that these psalms were "the hymns" that Paul and Silas were singing in that midnight hour. (Paul wrote about singing psalms and hymns and spiritual songs in Ephesians 5:19 and Colossians 3:16.)

If you check out the meaning of *hymn* or *hymns* in *Strong's Exhaustive Concordance*, you will find that "hymn" is the Greek word *humneo,* which is "to hymn, i.e. sing a religious ode; by impl. to celebrate (God) in song:—sing an hymn (praise unto)."[3] In Acts 16:25 where it says Paul and Silas *"sang praises"* (KJV), the word for "sang" is actually this same word for "hymn." "Hymns" then is the Greek word *humnos,* which is "a simpler (obsol.) form of *hudeo* (to celebrate)…a 'hymn' or religious ode (one of the Psalms):—hymn."[4]

I hate to disappoint you with this bit of information, but Paul and Silas probably were not singing a hymn that is found in our modern-day hymnals. There are a lot of good modern "hymns." There also are a lot of good contemporary "hymns" or worship songs. From *Strong's Exhaustive Concordance's* definitions, it is apparent that to celebrate God is what a hymn is to do. We also sing many songs today that do not qualify as a psalm, or hymn, or spiritual song.

What do the lyrics of our worship and praise songs say? I believe that the lyrics of a song are very important to God, especially when we are singing directly to Him in worship and praise. In my opinion, much recent contemporary Christian music and even worship and praise lyrical content is written out of human logic or religious thinking instead of out of our hearts responding to God's heart. I am beginning to wonder if God really does appreciate what we are saying about or to Him in some of our "hymns." I want what I sing to be written from the heart of a man or woman who loves the Lord.

When Paul wrote about *"psalms and hymns and spiritual songs"* in Ephesians 5 and Colossians 3, he added *"in your heart."* The heart is the inward you where the Spirit of God resides. The heart is the place where the new creation is.

Not only were Paul and Silas praying and singing, but while they were doing all that, the Bible also says that the prisoners were listening to them. The word translated as "listening" means "to listen with pleasure," as if listening to beautiful music.[5]

I believe these prisoners were probably pretty amazed at how these "Christians" were responding to the situation. In fact, I think that if these prisoners were enjoying the singing, then God was surely enjoying it as well. And it is highly possible that Paul and Silas were praying for the other prisoners and maybe even asked them to join in with them.

The Scriptures say that *"suddenly"* there was a great earthquake that shook even the foundations of the prison. I have heard it said that maybe God was enjoying the music so much that He decided to tap His foot, causing this great earthquake. Although that amuses us, the Bible does say that God *"inhabits the praises"* of His people (Psalm 22:3).

Anyway, this rescue was not like the one we saw in an earlier chapter where the Lord sent an angel. Instead of a manifestation of an angel, God sent a manifestation of His power that not only shook the foundation of the prison but also opened *all* the doors and loosed *all* the chains on everyone in the place—in addition to those of Paul and Silas!

In those times the jailer was responsible for the secure keeping of the prisoners. This jailer knew that he was a dead man if the prisoners escaped. The condition of his prison after the earthquake must have left no doubt in his mind that they had escaped, for he drew his sword to take his own life. But Paul shouted out to him, *"Do yourself no harm,"* telling him that all the prisoners were still there.

I believe that the Holy Spirit took control of the whole prison. Why else would the other prisoners not take off but stay right there? So after getting a light—probably some kind of torch—the jailer ran in and fell trembling before Paul and Silas. When God shows up, awesome things happen! When God's people pray and praise Him despite their circumstances, God always responds to their faith.

After bringing the prisoners out of the prison and, I believe, taking them all along to his house with him, the jailer asked Paul and Silas, *"Sirs, what must*

I do to be saved?" Talk about open doors! Not only were *all* the prison doors opened, but also the doors of the hearts of men were opened up! Paul and Silas responded by saying, *"Believe on the Lord Jesus Christ, and you will be saved, you and your household."*

Verse 32 of Acts 16 says that they spoke the word of the Lord to him (the jailer) *"and to all who were in his house."* That is what is supposed to happen in the lives of believers. No matter where we are, even when things are not looking too good, we are to be making prayers, supplications, intercessions and giving of thanks for all men, praising our God, singing to our God and then preaching the Word of the Lord to the people we find before us. This is God's will coming to pass in the earth!

Before the night was over, not only did the jailer's entire family believe on the Lord, but they also were all baptized. Thanks be to God, the jailer was still alive and rejoicing in his newfound salvation.

The Church's Midnight Hour

I believe that the church, the body of Christ—like Paul and Silas—is in its midnight hour. I believe that we are once again about to see a great earthquake—but this time it will be a supernatural earthquake. Satan has had his way for far too long! My Bible does not say that Satan has the victory. My Bible says that you and I have the victory in Christ! The apostle Paul got a revelation of who he was in Christ's victory and constantly wrote letters (our New Testament Scriptures) to his fellow ministers in the Gospel and to the churches throughout Europe and Asia so that they could know who they were in Christ's victory as well.

My Bible and yours says, *"For this purpose the Son of God was manifested, that He might destroy the works of the devil"* (1 John 3:8b). It also says, *"Inasmuch then as the children have partaken of flesh and blood, He Himself likewise shared in the same, that through death He might destroy him who had the power of death, that is, the devil"* (Hebrews 2:14). My Bible says over and over again that Jesus defeated Satan. It is our job, church, to see to it that God always gets the victory in all things!

If we begin "first of all" to put into action the charge we have been given to carry out, then our darkest hour could become our brightest hour. Like Paul's midnight hour experience, I believe that God will shake the foundations of the prisons. All the prisons in which Satan has held men and women captive will be shaken. All the doors will be opened. All the chains and bands will be broken off all prisoners. And men will cry out, "What must I do to be saved?"

This could be our finest hour if we will go God's way—the way of His Word. I encourage you to expect God to do great things in this generation. As seen in the book of Acts, not only did God set His men free, but He also, along with them, released all the other prisoners. Will God do the same today? I believe He will. I believe God is going to do a great work in the midnight hour.

Could this be the grand finale? The Bible says that God's will is for the church of Jesus Christ to be a glorious church! Not having spot or wrinkle or anything, but holy and without blemish! One that He loves, one that He gave Himself for, one that is being sanctified and cleansed with the washing of water by the word (Ephesians 5:25-27). God's desire is for all men to be saved and to come to the knowledge of the truth (1 Timothy 2:4).

I believe that God is going to shake the foundations of the nations (Haggai 2:7). I believe that God is going to break the chains and bondages that are holding back the people we are praying for, making supplications for, interceding for and giving thanks to Him for. He is going to save men and their whole households. God is not going to let Satan win the battle for the souls of men.

Here is something to think about. If Satan succeeded in taking with him to Hell 50 percent or more of all of the men and women God created in His own image and likeness, then would not Satan have ultimately beaten God the Father, God the Son and God the Holy Spirit? Here is one of Satan's biggest lies: —"Only a small number of people will be saved in the end." We have seen throughout this book that God's Word does not say that. And Hebrews 6:18 says that *"it is impossible for God to lie"*!

When we make intercession for men, Jesus is right there doing the same: Hebrews 7:25 says, *"Therefore He is also able to save to the uttermost those who come to God through Him, since He always lives to make intercession for them."*

He not only wants to save men and women, but He also wants to save them to the uttermost! Thank You, Jesus! It can't get any better than that.

Presently God is at work among the nations throughout the world. There is revival happening right now in many nations. It is time for the church to stop waiting on God; if you haven't figured it out by now, *He* is waiting on *us*.

Matthew 24:14 says, *"And this gospel of the kingdom will be preached in all the world as a witness to the nations, and then the end will come."* According to Jesus Himself, the end will come when the Gospel that He Himself proclaimed is preached in all the world. This "Gospel" is the Good News! This Gospel is that God is not out to get you or destroy you. God loves you despite where you are, who you are or what you are doing. This Gospel does not condemn you to Hell. This Gospel proclaims that you don't have to go there, that there is a way out—just believe on the Son, Jesus! This Gospel brings a message of hope to those who are lost, sick or oppressed by the devil. This Gospel, the one that Jesus preached, must once again be preached in all the world as a witness to the nations.

> *He* [Jesus] *said to His disciples, "The harvest truly is plentiful, but the laborers are few. Therefore pray the Lord of the harvest to send out laborers into His harvest."* Matthew 9:37-38

Church, let's rise up in this generation and fulfill that call.

Endnotes

1. W.E. Vine, *Vine's Expository Dictionary* (Nashville, Tennessee: Thomas Nelson Publishers, 1997), p. 571, *hymn.*
2. Earl D. Radmacher, gen. ed., *Nelson Study Bible,* New King James Version (Nashville, Tennessee: Thomas Nelson Publishers, 1997), p. 1001.
3. James Strong, *Strong's Exhaustive Concordance of the Bible* (Nashville, Tennessee: Holman Bible Publishers, n.d.), #G5214.
4. Strong, *Strong's Exhaustive Concordance,* #G5215.
5. Radmacher, *Nelson Study Bible,* p. 1851.

PART V

Commitment to the Charge

Chapter 16

When Jesus Comes, Will He Really Find Faith?

Then He spoke a parable to them, that men always ought to pray and not lose heart, saying: "There was in a certain city a judge who did not fear God nor regard man. Now there was a widow in that city; and she came to him, saying, 'Get justice for me from my adversary.' And he would not for a while; but afterward he said within himself, 'Though I do not fear God nor regard man, yet because this widow troubles me I will avenge her, lest by her continual coming she weary me.' " Then the Lord said, "Hear what the unjust judge said. And shall God not avenge His own elect who cry out day and night to Him, though He bears long with them? I tell you that He will avenge them speedily. Nevertheless, when the Son of Man comes, will He really find faith on the earth?" Luke 18:1-8

Preface to the Parable

Before telling this story of the "persistent widow," Jesus explained what it would be like on the earth when He returns in the Second Coming. Just before, in Luke 17, He spoke to the Pharisees and the others with Him about how it would be as in the days of Noah and in the days of Lot when He would come again.

In the days of Noah the people were eating, drinking and marrying. In the days of Lot they were eating, drinking, buying and selling, planting and building. Then suddenly change came and, with it, God's judgment was poured out on the unrighteous.

From what we can read in the Bible concerning the days of Lot and Noah, things were apparently going well economically and environmentally, and it will be the same in the days of Christ's return.

Spiritually speaking, things were not going well at all in the days of Noah and of Lot; likewise, it will not be going well before His return.

Keep in mind that God did not want to wipe out the people in the time of Noah. He gave them plenty of time to repent and get on board the boat with Noah and his family. They had many years to prepare themselves for the escape of the wrath to come while Noah built the ark.

In the case of the destruction of Sodom and Gomorrah in the days of Lot, God sent His angels into the city to see firsthand what was going on. Sadly, the people there had become so perverse that instead of looking for these messengers from God to find out how they could be saved, they pursued the angels so they could commit immoral sexual acts with them.

Before God released any judgment, He always sent out His messengers beforehand to warn people of the coming destruction. God does not change; I believe He will do the same before His judgment is poured out on the earth in the last day.

Jesus said, *"This gospel of the kingdom will be preached in all the world as a witness to all the nations, and then the end will come"* (Matthew 24:14).

The Gospel is the "Good News." The word *gospel* means "a good message" or "to announce good news."[1] So according to God, before the end comes the Good News that Jesus proclaimed will be preached as a witness (of Him, who is the Truth) to all the world first.

This Gospel, according to Jesus, can be summed up in one statement:

> *For God so loved the world that He gave His only begotten Son, that whoever believes in Him should not perish but have everlasting life. For God did not send His Son into the world to condemn the world, but that the world through Him might be saved.* John 3:16-17

Once again, it is *not* God's will for men to perish or be damned. Jesus was not sent here by the Father to condemn us, but to save us from eternal fire and to offer, through belief in Him, the promise of everlasting life.

The Good News is that you do not need to go to Hell or into everlasting destruction. The devil and all his demons already have been sentenced to eternal hellfire. They already are condemned by God—you are not! If you are not sure of your eternal destination, before you read any further, stop right now and say this prayer out loud before God:

> "Lord Jesus, I call upon You right now. I repent of all sin and all unrighteousness. I am turning from doing things my way and Satan's way. I believe in my heart that You came into this world to save all who would receive You. I confess You as the Lord of my life. I give all my past, all the present, and all my future plans to You now. I put all my past under the blood of the Lamb of God—Jesus. Lord Jesus, thank You for dying on the cross for me. Father God, thank You for raising Jesus from the dead. Thank You for saving me from Hell. Thank You for Your free gift of eternal life. Amen."

Getting saved is the greatest thing that can happen to any person; it is the greatest miracle! When we give our lives to Him, the Word of God says, *"Therefore, if anyone is in Christ, he is a new creation; old things have passed away; behold, all things have become new"* (2 Corinthians 5:17).

Many Christians have read and know this verse, which tells them they are "new creations." The very next words go on to say this to all believers:

> *Now all things are of God, who has reconciled us to Himself through Jesus Christ, and has given us the ministry of reconciliation, that is, that God was in Christ reconciling the world to Himself, not imputing their tres-*

passes to them, and has committed to us the word of reconciliation. Now then, we are ambassadors for Christ, as though God were pleading through us: we implore you on Christ's behalf, be reconciled to God. For He made Him who knew no sin to be sin for us, that we might become the righteousness of God in Him. 2 Corinthians 5:18-21

Christians, we all have a ministry given to us by God Himself, and that is *"the ministry of reconciliation."* He has ***"committed** to us **the word of reconciliation."*** The Word of God tells us that God is pleading through us to those who are lost without Him, "On Christ's behalf, be reconciled to God!" Jesus took sin on Himself, paying the price in full for our trespasses against God and for all our sin debt, so that we can be the righteousness of God in Jesus Christ!

Even though 2,000 years have past since Christ's first coming in the form of a man, God still loves the world just as much! He wants all people to know that it is His desire for them to know Him and to be made righteous (be in right standing with God) by faith in the Son, Jesus!

Never Give Up

So, what does this have to do with the persistent widow and the unrighteous judge? It has everything to do with it. In Luke 18:1, the Lord said that men ought to always pray and not lose heart (*"faint"* in the King James Version). In the charge we have been given in the Word of God we are told to make prayers, supplications, intercessions and giving of thanks for all men and for all who are in authority. Again the Scripture here is confirming that we need to always pray and, when we are praying, not to lose heart or faint. No matter how bad things get—even if or when things get as bad as they were in the days of Noah and Lot, we are to never quit or give up!

In this parable, Jesus said that there was a judge who did not fear God or regard (respect) man. This judge obviously was not the kind of a man a Christian would vote for in an election. It was bad enough that this judge did not respect man, the ones whom he should be helping in matters of justice, but he also had no fear of God. That means this man of authority was totally out to make decisions that ultimately satisfied his own well-being. This judge was on some type of ego trip to his own demise.

At first when the widow woman came to him pleading for help and asking him to get justice from her adversary, this judge would not help her. However, apparently this woman did not give up after her first, second, third or more visits to see this judge; she was persistent and kept on going back to see him with the same request over and over and over again.

Jesus said that this judge *"would not for a while; but afterward he said within himself, 'Though I do not fear God nor regard man, yet because this widow troubles me I will avenge her, lest by her continual coming she weary me' "* (Luke 18:4-5).

In verse 6 Jesus ended the story by making this very important statement about this judge's conclusion: *"Hear what the unjust judge said."*

Did you hear it? Did you hear what the unjust judge said? This widow woman came to him and continued to come to him for *"a while."* She did not give up; from what we can see in the Bible she did not change her request, she did not back down one bit; but she kept on coming back until the judge responded on her behalf.

This judge, even though he still had the same opinion concerning a fear of God and regard for men, said, *"Because this widow troubles me I will avenge her, lest by her continual coming she weary me."*

The Scriptures contain stories about some pretty amazing "widows." The widow in this parable appears to have been a real widow living in a real city, one whose real-life situation Jesus was totally aware of and was now using as an example of not giving up even when things were not looking any better.

Her persistence brought about change in her life. Even though the judge still remained the same, he grew weary of this woman and decided to help her.

This woman was a woman of faith. Even though things were not getting any better, even though this judge was not responding, she did not quit; she just kept on coming back until one day the unjust judge gave in.

Patience and Perseverance

In 1962 and 1963 the Supreme Court of the United States of America made some decisions that forever (maybe!) affected the lives of all citizens of the United States of America—that is, if there are no more "persistent widows" living in this generation. As we have seen in the life of Daniel, there are no man-made laws or decrees that are bigger than God Himself. Many times Christians have simply accepted what life has handed to them. Now it is time that we, with faith in our God, rise to the occasion! It is time for the people of God to stop being complacent and be those who through faith and patience receive the promises of God.

Did you notice that the widow woman did not attack the judge or jump up and down demanding her rights? She just kept on coming back until there was change. Persistence can bring about change. Ephesians 6:13 says, *"Take up the whole armor of God, that you may be able to withstand in the evil day, and having done all, to stand."* Don't sit down; even after you have done all, keep on standing!

Romans 5:3-4 says, *"...We also glory in tribulations, knowing that tribulation produces perseverance; and perseverance, character; and character, hope."*

Perseverance or patience working with faith always brings about results!

Hebrews 6:12 tells us to *"imitate those who through faith and patience inherit the promises."*

Faith and patience work together!

James 1:2-4 says, *"My brethren, count it all joy when you fall into various trials, knowing that the testing of your faith produces patience. But let patience have its perfect work, that you may be perfect and complete, lacking nothing."*

Speaking of Abraham, the Word of God says, *"After he had patiently endured, he obtained the promise"* (Hebrews 6:15).

Speaking of Job, the book of James says, *"Indeed we count them blessed who endure. You have heard of the perseverance of Job and seen the end intended by the Lord—that the Lord is very compassionate and merciful"* (James 5:11).

Do you have patience and perseverance at work in your life?

Do you have faith? If so, have patience working with it and you will receive God's promises. There are many folks (I used to be one of them) who have faith, but do not have patience at work with it.

I'm sure you have heard about the Christian who asked God to give him patience—and to hurry up! Have you noticed it doesn't come that way? Patience is a fruit of the Spirit, along with faith. God does give it to us, but we have to grow in it and, like a physical fruit, maintain and cultivate it in our lives.

Perseverance and patience will produce character in our lives. As has been said, we need more Christians with "character" instead of "characters" who are Christians.

Jesus Will Find Faith in Me!

> *And shall God not avenge His own elect who cry out day and night to Him, though He bears long with them? I tell you that He will avenge them speedily. Nevertheless, when the Son of Man comes, will He really find faith on the earth?* Luke 18:7-8

We saw from Jesus' parable that because of the widow woman's persistence, the unjust judge eventually came to her assistance and helped her after all.

In verse 7 Jesus went on to reveal the point of the parable. He said that our God, who *is* just, will avenge *"His own elect"* (referring to those of us who are His sons and daughters) if we cry out to Him day and night concerning the things we need Him to avenge us of in the world in which we live. I believe that if we *together* bring our requests to Him, He will respond to our prayers.

If we will heed the charge, if we will take those who are in positions of authority and the adverse decisions they have made that are against us before God, if we will continue in faith and patience—then God Himself will avenge us. He will come through for us. In fact, Jesus said that *"He will avenge them* ***speedily"***!

Are you presenting your case to Father God both day and night? By the way, doing so is not doubt and unbelief; it is real faith at work. This is the real deal. This is not "name it and claim it" or "blab it and grab it" theology. This is faith according to Jesus, who is God!

Can you imagine what will happen if multitudes of God's people begin to bring before Him political decisions or the government leaders themselves and cry out to Him to bring about change?

He will answer! He will avenge us! He will save men! He will save us—*if* we believe that He hears us when we pray.

The grand finale to this parable is this question Jesus asked: *"When the Son of Man comes, will He really find faith on the earth?"*

What a question; what a concluding thought. At first I wondered if He would find this kind of faith on the earth when He comes again. A lot of "faith teaching" has taken place over the years—I have taught it myself at times—but after a lot more researching of the Scriptures and after taking a long hard look and thinking out of this parable, I concluded that if Jesus wants to find this kind of faith at His coming, then there has to be some dramatic change in the hearts of Christians or He might be disappointed when He arrives.

It seems that we humans are very proficient at taking a good thing in the Word of God and running with it—many times to places that are not in line with the Scriptures, which is God's written will for us to live by.

I am happy to say that even though we (myself included) may have done some pretty stupid things with our "faith" at times in the past, with God's help we will in this generation take up the "shield of faith" and use it properly in our believing God to bring about His will and purposes in this earth.

I personally have made this decision concerning this faith: The Son of Man *will* find faith when He returns. *He will find it in me!* I am going to do things "according to the book"—His book. How about you? Will you be one in whom He can find faith?

It is time for a generation of God's people to begin to walk by faith and live by faith (2 Corinthians 5:7; Romans 1:17).

We are saints of God, and God says this about us in Revelation 13:10: *"Here is the patience and the faith of the saints."*

Yes, He will find faith in the earth when He comes! It is time for us to use our faith to see change come about in the lives of the "unjust judges" and those who do not fear God or respect man.

For with God all things are possible. Mark 10:27c

Ah, Lord GOD! Behold, You have made the heavens and the earth by Your great power and outstretched arm. There is nothing too hard for You. Jeremiah 32:17

Endnote

1. James Strong, *Strong's Exhaustive Concordance of the Bible* (Nashville, Tennessee: Holman Bible Publishers, n.d.), #G2098, #G2097.

Chapter 17

A Generation That Knows It Is More Blessed to Give Than to Receive

> *And remember the words of the Lord Jesus, that He said, "It is more blessed to give than to receive."* Acts 20:35b

The apostle Paul made this statement to the elders of the church at Ephesus when he was bidding them farewell. He was about to depart from Miletus and make his way to Jerusalem, as recorded in chapter 20 of the book of Acts.

These "elders" were the same group of men who received his epistle to the Ephesians, which we looked at in an earlier chapter pertaining to the instructions on the armor of God.

Paul told these men to remember these words of the Lord Jesus: *"It is more blessed to give than to receive."* Did you ever look for this quote in the four Gospels (Matthew, Mark, Luke and John)? Believe it or not, it isn't in them.

Jesus spoke many times of giving and of being blessed, but none of the writers of the Gospels included the line *"it is more blessed to give than to receive."*

Apparently this is something Paul himself received as a revelation from the Lord, something he must have heard Jesus saying to him.

Over the years I have come to discover that it *is* more blessed to give than to receive! I believe the whole reason God wants us to have an abundance of His blessings in the first place is so that we can then give to others. If you really want to get the blessings of God on your life, find someone to give to.

The Spiritual Law of Giving

In 2 Corinthians 9:6-8, Paul wrote to the Christians at Corinth concerning their giving in an offering that would be given to the saints at Jerusalem, who were going through some financially tough times. He told those involved in giving of their financial gifts:

> *But this I say: He who sows sparingly will also reap sparingly, and he who sows bountifully will also reap bountifully. So let each one give as he purposes in his heart, not grudgingly or of necessity; for God loves a cheerful giver. And God is able to make all grace abound toward you, that you, always having all sufficiency in all things, may have an abundance for every good work.*

As if that wasn't good enough, he went on to say this:

> *As it is written: "He has dispersed abroad, he has given to the poor; his righteousness endures forever." Now may He who supplies seed to the sower, and bread for food, supply and multiply the seed you have sown and increase the fruits of your righteousness, while you are enriched in everything for all liberality, which causes thanksgiving through us to God. For the administration of this service not only supplies the needs of the saints, but also is abounding through many thanksgivings to God.* 2 Corinthians 9:9-12

God has put spiritual laws into effect in the universe, and one of those spiritual laws is this: What and how you sow is what and how you will reap back in your life. As the Scriptures say right here in 2 Corinthians 9, if you sow sparingly, then that is exactly how you will reap: sparingly. But if you sow bountifully, you also will reap bountifully.

In other words, if you want a little blessing, give a little one. If you want a large blessing, give a big one.

Can you see in these verses that it is God's will for us to *"have an abundance for every good work"*? God gives the seed; we do our part and sow it or plant it into the life of someone else; then God Himself multiplies it back into our lives. Then we can sow again—over and over. It is more blessed to give than to receive!

I believe that this spiritual law also works in the realm of praying for others.

In Luke 6:38 Jesus said, *"Give, and it will be given to you: good measure, pressed down, shaken together, and running over will be put into your bosom. For with the same measure that you use, it will be measured back to you."*

We often use this verse as a reference in giving money into others' lives or ministries. But giving is a Godly principle that works in whatever area it is used, be it in money, or love, or time, or even in judging others, as the preceding verse, Luke 6:37, says.

I believe that when we give of our lives in prayer for others, it will likewise bring about prayer made for us. Did you know that in the book of Hebrews it says Jesus is *"able to save to the uttermost those who come to God through Him, since He always lives to make intercession for them"* (Hebrews 6:25)?

Jesus, our High Priest in Heaven, wants to save us to the uttermost! And He Himself is interceding and praying for you and I right now!

I don't know why we spend so much of our time praying for and about ourselves. If we can get beyond our own concerns and pray for others, I believe we will begin to see the benefits of Jesus' praying for you and I.

Have you ever noticed that even "The Lord's Prayer" that Jesus taught His disciples uses the words *our* and *us* over and over again rather than *me* and *I* (Matthew 6:9-13)?

Good Measure

Jesus said, *"Give, and it will be given to you: good measure, pressed down, shaken together, and running over will be put into your bosom."* When Jesus used the phrase *"good measure,"* He was referring to how, in the marketplace, grain was poured out, shaken down and filled to overflowing so that the buyer received the full amount purchased. Such is the full measure or "good measure" that will be returned to the one who has been generous.[1]

As we saw earlier when studying the armor of God, God wants us to be praying in the Spirit for all the saints. I believe that if you and I will sow our time and effort into prayer for others, then God Himself will see to it that someone empowered by the Holy Spirit prays for us. In fact, it is Jesus praying for us through the Spirit working in them. You see, God is not raising up a bunch of spoiled brats in His family. He is moving us from a place of selfishness and self-seeking to a place where we can be truly "blessed" in Him.

It is the desire of the Spirit of God to get us beyond praying from "head knowledge" to where we can "let go and let God" work through and in our prayers.

The theme of this book is this charge and this generation. Can you carry out this charge in this generation? Do you want a quiet and peaceful life in all reverence and godliness? If so, first of all, pray, make supplications, intercede and give thanks to God—for others! Not only for yourself.

It is time to get past the "what's in it for me" attitude. Jesus did not tell you and I to *"seek first the kingdom of* [insert your name]*...and all these things shall be added to you"* (Matthew 6:33). He didn't leave it up to us to fill in the blank in our Bibles. It is God's kingdom we are supposed to be seeking first. This is not a "once and done" deal. No, this is something that we continue to do every day of our lives! Just because you "sought first the kingdom of God" five, ten, or even twenty years ago, it doesn't mean that you are done seeking it now. And when you look at the context of this verse, Jesus was telling His followers that all the things the Gentiles were seeking or chasing after would be added to us if we would just do things His way.

Are you discovering in your life that it is more blessed to give than to receive?

Start giving. Start blessing others. Do the charge that God gave to us the church. And as you do, watch God begin the multiplying in your life.

Endnote

1. Earl D. Radmacher, gen. ed., *Nelson Study Bible,* New King James Version (Nashville, Tennessee: Thomas Nelson Publishers, 1997), p. 1703.

Chapter 18

Committed to the Charge

First of all that supplications, prayers, intercessions, and giving of thanks be made for all men, for kings and all who are in authority, that we may lead a quiet and peaceable life in all godliness and reverence. For this is good and acceptable in the sight of God our Savior, who desires all men to be saved and to come to the knowledge of the truth. 1 Timothy 2:1-4

Now that we know the charge given to the church, we as believers in the Word of God must *commit* ourselves to keeping it and carrying it out.

This charge I commit to you, son Timothy. 1 Timothy 1:18a

And the things that you have heard from me among many witnesses, commit these to faithful men who will be able to teach others also. 2 Timothy 2:2

O Timothy! Guard what was committed to your trust, avoiding the profane and idle babblings and contradictions of what is falsely called knowledge—

by professing it some have strayed concerning the faith. Grace be with you. Amen. 1 Timothy 6:20-21

Be Committed

What we have learned in this book is the will of God for us. If we will do these things, God will see to it that we have a quiet and peaceable life, exactly as He has told us in the Scriptures. He is the one who said it by His Spirit and He is the one who wrote the book! His word to us is, *"For this is good and acceptable in the sight of God our Savior"*!

We must do our part and perform these things that have been committed to the church. The apostle Paul committed these things to Timothy, Timothy was to commit these things to faithful men and the faithful men were to teach others.

Because of the Holy Spirit's preservation of the written Scriptures throughout the ages right up until the present, we can receive the same words and commit ourselves to them in this age.

In the world that we live in, "commitment" is lacking. Even in the body of Christ, commitment is lacking in many areas. It is very apparent that the world has and is affecting the church. Meanwhile, God's will is that we (the church) be affecting the world for the good. We are the salt of the earth (Matthew 5:13)!

In whatever area we have failed in our commitments to the church, to one another or to the Lord and His Word, we need to repent and get back on track in going forward in Christ.

We need to put under the blood of Jesus every commitment we have ever broken in our lives and ask the Lord to come and empower us by His Spirit to trust in Him and commit ourselves to Him and His Word!

First Timothy 6:20, quoted at the beginning of this chapter, says to *"guard what was committed to your trust."* Not only are we to commit and teach these things to others, but we also must guard them. The Scripture says that the way we guard them is by avoiding profane and idle babblings and contradictions.

Jesus told us in Mark 4 that Satan comes immediately to steal the Word of God when it is sown in our hearts. The good news is that he cannot steal the

Word from those people who receive the Word sown in *"good ground."* Having good ground is evidenced by a person hearing the Word, accepting it and bearing fruit (Mark 4:20). God wants you and I to have good ground in our hearts. God wants us to have the fruit of His Word to come forth 30-, 60- and 100-fold.

Satan would rather Christians be fruitless. That's not a new desire on his part. Satan not only stole the fruit in the lives of God's first man and woman, but he also took away the whole garden in which God had placed them in. How did he accomplish that? He enticed them into disobeying God's charge to them.

Adam failed by not guarding the charge God had given to him, which was to maintain the Garden of Eden. Are you committed to the charge God has given to His church? Are you guarding all that He has committed to your trust?

At the time Paul wrote to Timothy and the church, there were *"profane and idle babblings and contradictions"* of what was God's knowledge (His written Word). Such contradictions are present today and will continue to try to rob us of the truth if we are not careful.

The thing we have to do is guard the truth we have found in the Word of God and avoid all those things that Satan (or Satan using men or women) will bring our way to contradict what God has entrusted to us.

Restoration of the Charge in This Generation

I am committing myself to His charge! I will make supplications, prayers, intercessions and giving of thanks for all men, for kings and all who are in authority, with the help of the Holy Spirit of God. I will do this for Him and I will do this for you. My prayer is that you will join with me and do the same for me, in our commitment to the charge that was given us a long time ago.

I believe that God is restoring in this generation that which He exhorted us to do *"first of all."* Why? It is God's will for you and I to live out lives that are quiet and peaceful. Can you say this with the psalmist, David:

> *The LORD is my shepherd; I shall not want. He makes me to lie down in green pastures; He leads me beside the still waters. He restores my soul; He leads me in the paths of righteousness for His name's sake. Yea, though I walk through the valley of the shadow of death, I will fear no evil; for You*

> *are with me; Your rod and Your staff, they comfort me. You prepare a table before me in the presence of my enemies; you anoint my head with oil; my cup runs over. Surely goodness and mercy shall follow me all the days of my life; and I will dwell in the house of the* L*ORD forever.* Psalm 23

Enjoying a quiet and peaceable life in all reverence and godliness is not some "New Age theology" or "false concept." It is nothing less than the will of God for His children. Don't believe any of Satan's lies! Satan will always, always contradict what God has said in the Bible. Psalm 23 was, is and always will be the Word of God for His people. Jesus, the Good Shepherd, came that we may have abundant life:

> *I have come that they may have life, and that they may have it more abundantly.* John 10:10b

We are the *"they"* He spoke of. So according to His Word, we *"may"* have life and we *"may"* have it more abundantly. Did you ever notice that this verse does not say that they *shall* have life and that they *shall* have it more abundantly?

I believe that Jesus deliberately left His message concerning abundant life in this way. He wanted us to know that we do not automatically experience abundance in our lives just because we are "Christians." We have to believe and know that it is God's will for us and then pursue Him and all His commandments or charges that He has given us in the New Covenant Scriptures. The Good Shepherd laid down His life for the sheep (John 10:11); now we must lay down our lives for Him and the purpose of the Gospel. Now we must respond to others the way Jesus would.

Speaking of Jesus, the apostle Peter wrote, *"Who, when He was reviled, did not revile in return; when He suffered, He did not threaten, but committed Himself to Him who judges righteously"* (1 Peter 2:23). Speaking to the church, he said, *"All of you be of one mind, having compassion for one another; love as brothers, be tenderhearted, be courteous; not returning evil for evil or reviling for reviling, but on the contrary blessing, knowing that you were called to this, that you may inherit a blessing"* (1 Peter 3:8-9).

We are not to return evil for evil or retaliate in the same way that others mistreat us. The Scripture says, *"on the contrary,"* we are to bless those who do us wrong. This is our "calling" from God; we are to always choose to bless. In this we will inherit a blessing from God.

Do you want to be blessed? Make supplications and pray and intercede for and give thanks to God for *all* men. Commit yourself to the Father as Jesus Himself did. Commit your will to His will. Commit to the charge that was given—and you will be blessed.

Will you rise up in this generation?

After these things I looked, and behold, a great multitude which no one could number, of all nations, tribes, peoples, and tongues, standing before the throne and before the Lamb, clothed with white robes, with palm branches in their hands, and crying out with a loud voice, saying, "Salvation belongs to our God who sits on the throne, and to the Lamb!"

Revelation 7:9-10

APPENDIX A

Putting the Charge Into Action

But be doers of the word, and not hearers only, deceiving yourselves. For if anyone is a hearer of the word and not a doer, he is like a man observing his natural face in a mirror; for he observes himself, goes away, and immediately forgets what kind of man he was. But he who looks into the perfect law of liberty and continues in it, and is not a forgetful hearer but a doer of the work, this one will be blessed in what he does. James 1:22-25

As we can see from these verses, we are to be not only hearers of the Word of God, but also doers of what we heard from the Word. After looking into the *"perfect law of liberty,"* we must continue in it and carry it out in our lives.

God wants you and I to be truly blessed by Him. His Word says that the one who not only hears but does the Word of the Lord, *"this one will be blessed in what he does."*

Do you want to be blessed by Father God? Then begin to do all that He is revealing to you from His Word.

Acting on the Word

All of what is contained in this book will be worthless concerning the kingdom of God unless you and I put into action what we have learned.

I want you to know that I am in the same place as you are in this. I have learned a lot studying, researching, praying, meditating and writing *This Charge... This Generation.* Now I, like you, must commit myself to the charge given to the church and be a doer of the Word. I have to be one who practices what I preach!

Therefore, following are a few examples of how to bring supplications, prayers, intercessions and giving of thanks to God for all men, for kings and all who are in authority. Remember Abraham's steps of faith that we looked at in Chapter 10? See if you can see these steps used in these examples.

EXAMPLE #1

For All Men or One in Authority (Unsaved)

> Father God, I come to You on behalf of (*insert name*). Father, according to Your Word it is Your will for all men to be saved and come to the knowledge of the truth. So according to Your own will, Your Word, I bring this person to you right now. I believe that Your Word is true and that You desire to see (*name*) in Your kingdom. Even though he/she appears to be destined for Hell, Lord, I ask in faith, right now, that You bring about change in his/her life by the power of the Holy Spirit. Lord, I ask that You send ambassadors of the good news of Jesus Christ into (*name*)'s life so that he/she can hear the Gospel message and receive it in his/her heart today.
>
> Father, You are God; You give life to the dead and You call those things that do not exist as though they did. I agree with Your Word right now

concerning (*name*). Give life to (*name*) where there is death now by Your Spirit.

I believe by faith in what You have said in Your Word. I glorify You for what you are doing in (*name*) from this day forward. Thank You for saving him/her from sin, Hell and the devil. Thank You for the work that You are doing in (*name*)'s life. Amen.

EXAMPLE #2

For All Men or One in Authority (Doing Evil)

Father God, I come to You on the behalf of (*insert name*). Although it appears that he/she is far from doing things in a way that would please You, I choose to make supplications, prayers, intercessions and giving of thanks for (*name*) as You have told us to do in the charge given to Your church. Lord, by Your Spirit I ask that You bring about all the changes necessary in (name)'s life so that we as Your people can continue to live out lives that are quiet and peaceable in all godliness and reverence, which You Yourself have told us in Your Word is good and acceptable to You. Father, bring truth where there is deception and lies. Bring light where there is darkness. Bring salvation where there is death. You have said in Your Word that when the enemy comes in like a flood You will lift up a standard against them.

So, Father, contrary to what I see in the realm of the natural, I choose to come into agreement with You and Your Word. Like Daniel, I believe that You are the God who delivers and rescues and that You are able to deliver me, a servant of the Most High God, from the mouth of the lions or even the devil himself as a roaring lion.

Father, by faith in Your Word, I choose to bless (*name*) rather than speak evil of him/her. I call (*name*) saved by the blood of Jesus Christ; I call (*name*) one who makes good and Godly decisions.

I thank You, Lord, that right now You are bringing about change in (*name*)'s life. I thank You that You are bringing truth and Godly counsel to him/her in his/her heart and soul. I thank You that You are saving him/her as well as those who influence him/her in his/her decisions right now by Your own mighty intervention with Your Holy Spirit at work in this situation. Father, I glorify Your name and I glorify You for all that You are doing in (*name*) now. Amen.

EXAMPLE #3

For All Men or One in Authority (Who Kills the Innocent)

Father God, I come to You on behalf of (*insert name*). Father, despite what I see, hear, feel, smell or even taste, I choose to respond to the situation at hand in a way that is pleasing to You.

I have found out, according to Your very own Word, which is the truth, that it is Your will for all men—including this man/woman—to be saved and come to the knowledge of the truth. Also, it is written in Your Word that it is Your desire that no one perish but that all—including (*name*)—receive the free gift of salvation that is only found in Your Son, Jesus.

Father, I ask that as You did in the life of Saul of Tarsus, send forth Your angel, or even Jesus Himself, and stop this man/woman in what he/she is doing. Reveal truth to (*name*) and bring the evil deeds being done by him/her to an end. Bring the glorious light of the Gospel where there is darkness. Save (*name*) to the uttermost as You have saved me. I realize that I too was without Christ and lost, deceived and blinded by darkness, just like everyone who is not redeemed by the blood of Jesus. So, Father, as You have saved me, save (*name*) today by the power of Your Holy Spirit. Deliver (*name*) from the power of darkness that is controlling and influencing him/her.

> I believe that You are saving (*name*) now and performing all the changes necessary to bring about life.
>
> I thank You for saving (*name*) and for all that You are doing in bringing about change for the good in him/her and in the lives of all with him/her and influencing him/her now.
>
> I glorify You, for not only do You hear my prayer but You also answer the prayers of the saints when we pray according to Your Word. Let Your kingdom come and let Your will be done on earth as it is in Heaven. Amen.

After praying or bringing this person or situation to the Father, ask the Holy Spirit to use you and your words to intercede or make intercession by praying in the Spirit for them.

The Holy Spirit knows exactly what is going on in that person's life and can cause your prayers to be according to that good, perfect and acceptable will of God.

Keep in mind that doing this is not a once and for all done deal. Remember the persistent widow? Remember Abraham? Continually bring your supplications and prayers to Father God. Make intercession for the person and give thanks to God for him or her until the breakthrough or change comes. Such transformation could be accomplished in one hour, one day, one week, one month or even longer. Do not quit. Do not give up. Do not let go. Watch and pray! Having done all, stand.

By faith agree with God; fight against the devil and the powers of darkness and always bless.

Be a doer as well as a hearer of the Word.

Right after James wrote that admonition, he said this: *"If anyone among you thinks he is religious, and does not bridle his tongue but deceives his own heart, this one's religion is useless"* (James 1:26).

We must bridle our tongues. In other words, we must stop saying everything that comes to our minds. We must only speak forth words that come from the heart—words that are pleasing to the Lord, words that are in agreement with what God Himself would say.

Many times we respond with words that are contrary to the Word of God. When we do this, we deceive our own hearts, the Scripture says. Our heart is where the born-again spirit man resides. Our heart is the place where the Holy Spirit of God abides in us. We must respond out of what is in the heart, or else our religion is useless.

This is My Prayer for You

Father God, for the many times that we have deceived our own hearts by not bridling our tongues, forgive us. Forgive us of all the times we collectively and individually did not respond to others according to Your Word. Forgive us of the many times we did Satan's will by accusing the brethren instead of praying for them, and thereby fighting against the true enemy, the devil and the powers of darkness.

Forgive us for not carrying out Your charge to pray for all men, for kings, for all who are in authority so that we, the body of Christ, can live out lives that are quiet and peaceable in all reverence and godliness.

Empower us as believers in this generation by Your Holy Spirit to do the charge that the apostle Paul by Your Spirit exhorted us to do "first of all" once again.

Let the people of God declare, as the multitude of angels did 2,000 years ago at the coming of our Savior, "Glory to God in the highest, and on earth peace, goodwill toward men!" In Jesus' name, amen.

APPENDIX B

Who Are the Authorities in My Life?

Don't be ignorant of who the men and women are in positions of authority in your life. Find out who these folks are and carry out the charge concerning them. Bring them and their doings before Father God; make supplications, prayers and intercessions for them. Pray in the Spirit for them. And give thanks to God for what He is doing and going to do in their lives. "Prayer changes things" is more than a nice cliché!

Government Leaders

President/King/Queen/Emperor ____________________

Vice-President/Prime Minister ____________________

Senators & Congressmen ____________________

____

____

Supreme Court Justices ______________________

____

____

____

____

State Court Justices ______________________

____

____

____

Your State:

Governor ______________________

State Senators ______________________

State Legislators ______________________

City/Town Mayor ______________________

City/Town Council Members ______________________

____

____

____

City/Town Sheriff ______________________

City/Town Deputies ______________________

____

____

City/Town Chief of Police ______________________

City/Town Police Officers ______________________

____

____

____

School District Superintendent ______________________

School Principal ______________________

School Board Members ______________________

____

____

University President ______________________

Professors ______________________

____

Other Local Authorities ______________________

____

____

Military Leaders

Commander in Chief ______________________

Secretary of Defense ______________________

Leading Generals ______________________

____

____

Other Leaders, as appropriate ______________________

____

____

____

Church Leaders

Senior Pastor ______________________

Assistant Pastor(s) ______________________

____

Elders ______________________

____

____

____

Deacons ______________________

____

____

Apostles ______________________

Prophets ______________________

Evangelists ______________________

Teachers ______________________

Other Ministry Leaders ______________________

____

____

____

____

Others ______________________________

____

____

____

____

____

Obviously these lists are not all-inclusive. Simply use them as a guide. Once you know the names of those who are in positions of authority, let the Lord use you in praying for them. Use Scripture to base your petitions and requests on. Remember that there are no limits to what can be done for all men, for kings and for all who are in authority. Also, do not pray for only those people who directly affect your life and family. Pray for others who have influence in our society. (i.e. directors, producers, entertainment and media professionals.) Pray also for the saints who are suffering persecution around the globe. Pray for the world leaders who are presently opposing the Christian church and the Gospel message of Jesus Christ. Young people and children, pray for your parents.

Remember, *"we do not wrestle against flesh and blood, but against principalities, against powers, against the rulers of the darkness of this age, against spiritual hosts of wickedness in the heavenly places"* (Ephesians 6:12). Pray for ungodly kings, presidents and emperors as well as Godly ones. God desires for all to be saved. Just think what God could do in a nation or nations when He changes the heart of a man who influences a multitude of souls. By the way, He is doing that very thing right now throughout the world because He is restoring the charge given in this generation!

AUTHOR'S NOTE:

Faith Does Not Call Things That Are As Though They Do Not Exist!

This is where many believers have gone down the wrong road in their "faith" confession.

The Bible/God's Word does not say that God "calls the things that are as though they do not exist." God is not a magician. God did not give Abraham a Rabbit Foot or a Magic Wand so that he could wave it over his wife and... "poof" ... there's a boy with her.

Many times there are sicknesses and problems happening in our lives and we want God to just wave His Magic Wand over our lives and in a flash all of it is gone. Did you ever stop to think that if there is something bad happening in your life that maybe — possibly there could be something that needs to be corrected in your life or even stopped that could be the reason why this problem exists in the first place?

Here is a real life example: I could have the flu. I do not say, "by faith, I do not have the flu." That would be calling the things that are as though they do not exist. That would be a form of mind over matter. That would be more of a form of witchcraft than a "Christian" practice.

This is what God's faith would say, "Yes, I do have the flu, but God's Word says that I am healed by the stripes of Jesus. I am agreeing with what God says about me." It is not God's Will for any of us to have the flu.

Also while we are talking about it the way that God Himself would, maybe we ought to take the time to see if there is a reason why we got the flu in the first place. There are many Christians that are breaking natural laws or spiritual laws, sometimes both spiritual and natural laws at the same time and then they expect God to fix everything, despite all that they have done.

Did you know that 1 Corinthians 11:29-32 says that *many* are weak and sick and are dying in the Church because of taking the Communion elements in an unworthy manner? James 5:14 says that if there are sick in the Church to let them call for the elders of the Church to have them pray over them and anoint them with oil in the name of the Lord. The next verse goes on to say that if the one being prayed for has committed any sins he will be forgiven. Many times sin in our lives leaves an open door for the destroyer. I believe that Christians need to have the God kind of faith — faith that calls things that are not as though they do exist, and also we need to have good "common sense" as well.

Are you going to do the things that Abraham did to bring about the promises of God? Or will you try doing it some other way? Do you remember the list of the steps of faith that we looked at that brought to pass the Will of God in Abraham's life?

Printed in the United States
24882LVS00005BA/4-24

9 780976 380009